D1547733

Eternal Life

Other books available
from Sophia Institute Press
by Romano Guardini:

The Lord's Prayer
The Rosary of Our Lady
Learning the Virtues That Lead You to God
Preparing Yourself for Mass
The Art of Praying
The Living God

Romano Guardini

Eternal Life

What You Need to Know
About Death, Judgment,
and Life Everlasting

SOPHIA INSTITUTE PRESS®
Manchester, New Hampshire

Eternal Life: What You Need to Know About Death, Judgment, and Life Everlasting was published in 1940 and in 1966 by Werkbund-Verlag, Würzburg, Germany, under the title *Die Letzten Dinge: Die christliche Lehre vom Tode, der Läuterung nach dem Tode, Auferstehung, Gericht und Ewigkeit*. Pantheon Books in New York published an English translation in 1954. This 1998 edition by Sophia Institute Press uses Pantheon's 1954 translation by Charlotte E. Forsyth and Grace B. Branham, entitled *The Last Things*, with slight revisions to that text.

The cover painting is a detail of *The Annunciation*, by Roger van der Weyden (c. 1399-1464), in the Louvre, Paris (Superstock).

Sophia Institute Press®
Box 5284, Manchester, NH 03108
1-800-888-9344

Nihil Obstat: Herman Branderis, *Censor Librorum*
Imprimatur: Peter L. Ireton, Bishop of Richmond
Richmond, Virginia, January 18, 1954

Library of Congress Cataloging-in-Publication Data

Guardini, Romano, 1885-1968.
  [Letzten Dinge. English]
  Eternal life: what you need to know about death, judgment, and
life everlasting / Romano Guardini.
       p.   cm.
  "This 1998 edition by Sophia Institute Press uses Pantheon's
1954 translation by Charlotte E. Forsyth and Grace B. Branham,
entitled The last things, with slight revisions to that text"—T.p.
verso.
  ISBN 0-918477-69-7 (pbk. : alk. paper)
  1. Eschatology. 2. Catholic Church—Doctrines. I. Guardini,
Romano, 1885-1968. Last things. II. Title.
BT821.G8213   1998
236—DC21   97-51872 CIP

98 99 00 01 02 10 9 8 7 6 5 4 3 2 1

Contents

Foreword

It is by time that life is made actual. In this conditioning by time, three divisions appear not only clearly but decisively: the beginning, the end, and the present moment. The beginning and the end mark the limits of existence as a whole. In the moment, existence gathers itself, approaches the living man, gives itself into his hands, and from his free decision receives its permanent meaning.

If understood according to the gospel, these three divisions of time furnish the fundamental principles of a Christian doctrine concerning existence in time. The beginning: about each man's beginning and about the beginning of the world in which man lives and which fulfills itself in man. The end: about the conclusion of each man's life, and about the end of the world that is ordered with reference to man. Finally, the moment: about time becoming the present in its fleeting course, thereby entrusting existence to man in irrevocable, unalterable, unique fashion—that is, his own existence and that of the world related to him. If we apply and extend the usual terminology, these three divisions of the Christian doctrine concerning existence in time are called archelogy, eschatology, and kairology.[1]

In this study, I shall try to outline what Christianity teaches concerning the end and that which pertains to it—death, resurrection, purification after death, the Last Judgment, and eternal life.

It is, in fact, only an outline. I am not aiming to present an exhaustive survey, but rather to focus on certain points from which the subject may appear more definite and intelligible. Christian eschatology discusses things which in part are very remote from modern sensibility. The changes wrought in our view of the universe and in our sensation of life have given rise, on these points especially, to much questioning and opposition. Instead of treating the subject in the fullest manner, then, I shall confine myself to establishing a relationship between the timeless teaching of Revelation and our present spiritual and intellectual situation.

Romano Guardini
Berlin, Advent 1940

---

[1]The study of first things (*arche*, the beginning), of last or final things (*eschatos*, last), and of the time in between (*kairos*, the moment).

Eternal Life

What death is

Death was not meant to be

In the short space of this first chapter something will be said of the Christian teaching about death—a great theme not easy to exhaust. It will be in place, therefore, to bring out at once the sharp differences between the Christian view of death and current notions.

Paul says in his letter to the Romans, "Through one man sin entered into the world and through sin death, and thus death has passed unto all men because [in that first man] all have sinned."[2]

The modern reader is inclined to accept the passage in a fairly general sense—either in the ethical sense: that the first man did wrong, and by so doing injured himself and his posterity radically; or in the vaguely religious sense: that in forsaking God, the first man destroyed the life of the soul, or something of the sort. In reality, the passage means precisely what it says. That it does so appears with particular clearness when it is set

[2]Rom. 5:12.

beside another important passage on death, in the second chapter of Genesis: "And the Lord God took man, and put him into the paradise of pleasure to dress it and to keep it. And He commanded him, saying, 'Of every tree of paradise, thou shalt eat, but of the tree of the knowledge of good and evil, thou shalt not eat. For in what day soever thou shalt eat of it thou shalt die the death.' "[3] Paul merely follows what was said in Genesis, and both passages express the same thing: that man, originally, and in the intention of his Creator, should not have died.

To the modern reader this statement is little short of nonsense. He has been taught by science to regard death as a natural necessity and in consequence to look on death as a natural part of life. Indeed, in recent decades an attitude has grown up about which much could be said, and which virtually amounts to a surrender to death. A protest is in order, for although Revelation is a mystery, it is not a fairy tale. It is divine truth, transcending reason, but still truth. Consciences must not suppose that they may be forced by divine authority to accept nonsense, and Christians should perceive that they have been admitted to a higher view than that of natural science, which, although mysterious, is yet real.

∞

Death is the last part of human life. But for everything alive it is this last part which is crucial. Our nature is patterned on a process in which the end is part of the whole. This end is

---

[3]Gen. 2:15-17. The biblical references in these pages are based on the Douay-Rheims edition of the Old and New Testaments.

not like the last few drops poured out of a cup to signify that there is no more. The end determines all that precedes it. There is a proverb, "All's well that ends well." The obvious meaning is that if the end turns out happy, the rest will come right somehow. But in a deeper sense, if the end comes right, it is through the concurrence of the whole, and in a good ending the whole acquires its validity. It is in the last notes that a melody is first present as a whole. In a play, it is not until the outcome that the hero's character is fully illumined. So, too, death brings man's life to its fulfillment—for good or ill. How, then, can Paul say that had there been no sin, there would have been no death?

The answer is first that certainly there had to be an end. The shape of our life requires a conclusion to give it its final validity. But this end would not have been death as we know it.

Death cannot be explained naturally

If the end of human life would not have been death as we know it, what, then, would it have been?

Death is not merely an appendix to life in the manner of the ending of a bad play whose ending could never be predicted. Death is built into life's structure, and issues from its course. It is present long before the conclusion, actually throughout the whole development of life. Life has been defined as a movement directed toward death. How, then, can death be said not to be necessary? To answer with reflection, let us set before our eyes, in all its mighty power, this thing called death.

Its foundation lies in what, by a figure of speech, may be called physical death. Everything, even in the inanimate world, has form and shape. Nothing exists as a mere series of acts or as clusters of qualities. And every form decays. Some are transitory like the waves; some, like crystals or mountain-ranges or heavenly bodies, last over a long period of time. But sooner or later all disintegrate.

Eternal Life

In its literal meaning, death applies only to things that have life. Biological death means the failure of the constructive powers to maintain themselves. Wastes are not eliminated, enemies not held at bay. Death is the final result of a change in the inner economy, a result which starts to take shape when life begins.

There is such a thing also as psychological death. A man may put up a defense against death, as everything alive has to defend itself, and yet not resist it in his heart. In the end he will no longer wish to live. He finds no satisfaction in living. Life is not worth the trouble. Again, such an outcome was present from the first, for the psychic nature is ever in the process of dying.

Childhood—in a way, a complete life in itself—perishes to make way for youth, and youth comes to an end at maturity. Life as a whole is not a uniform sequence. It consists of diverse and self-contained forms, and each must give way so that the next may find a place. So different are these various portions of our lives that often we cannot think ourselves back into our own past. Or we may go back to some cherished experience—a landscape, a book, a friend—and find that we no longer respond to it. Something has died. If we look closer we see that the character of man's relation to life is contradictory. He wills to live, but he wills also to die. It is the will to die which manifests itself in that puzzling inclination people have to cause themselves pain, to alienate their friends, or to injure their own work. All such unintelligible behavior is a form of psychological dying. And how far it prevails depends only on our inner power of defense.

There is, lastly, another form of death that may be called biographical. Each man's life is built around certain settled motives of action. These motives, for some reason, may cease to be, and no new ones come up to supply their place. A woman, for instance, may be married, have children, and manage a household. Then her children grow up, leave home, and start families of their own. The woman is no longer indispensable. If she is not able to take up some other activity or fill her leisure from her own inner resources, her life, biographically speaking, is over. Its natural shape is complete, finished. What remains is to come to terms with the fact.

Or take a man who has thrown himself into his work with everything there is in him. The day comes when he perceives that out of loyalty to the work itself, he must resign and hand it over to someone better fitted to do it than he is. Unless he finds something to do that makes it worth his while to begin afresh, or can put his leisure to intellectual or social use, his life, viewed as a biography, is finished, however long it may linger on in fact.

We might go on, but enough has been said to show how heavily death weighs upon life as a whole and upon each instant of it. What is to be done about it?

∞

There have been numerous attempts at a solution. Let us begin with what the positivists say. Positivism, the philosophy prevalent among the so-called practical men, and much under the influence of science and technology, views death as a merely natural occurrence. Man is a living being; he is like all the rest except that he is more highly organized. Whatever has life must fall into decay. Death is part of the natural order. Man must see it for what it is, and endure what cannot be altered. Let him accept it high-mindedly, or with courage, or with resignation—at the very least, with decency.

The answer of idealism is at the other extreme. Being rather a feeling than an opinion, it is hard to put into words. The hero struggles, fails, suffers, and at last goes down in sublime defeat. We are made to feel that in his ruin all guilt is atoned for. A vista opens up, and a glorious light streams in. All that is corruptible has fallen away; the essential core, however, lives on in imperishable light. This is a view that does not bear close inspection, and therefore should be kept a little vague. In the thought of idealism, whatever is nobly lived or nobly done endures forever. But if the idealist is pressed with the *why* and the *wherefore*, no plain answer is forthcoming. This is a faith that leaves a lingering doubt as to its confidence in its own profession.

Somewhere between these two extremes lies a third answer. It says that all things come to an end, life included, and that is how it should be. To wish to go on living beyond the end is folly; it is also unmanly and dishonorable. The very inevitability of the end makes life great and glorious. Death actually is part of life itself, its obverse, its countermovement, its high peak, its excess. It will be mastered by being accepted with a firm mind, or, better still, with fervor and, as the final fulfillment of life, by being itself "lived."

Our natural feeling, if we set the fact of death accurately before ourselves, is that all these answers do not ring true.

They do not correspond to the whole of reality, but only to some partial aspect of it. They do not face the real issue squarely; they sidestep it, either by adopting a seeming matter-of-factness or a spurious spirituality, or an extravagant affirmation of life. The truth is different. The last thing is not death, but life.

The answer given by religion among various peoples and in all ages is full of this consciousness, that not death but life is final. With the single exception of Buddhism in its southern form, they seem to answer the question concerning death with the intuition of eternity. Upon closer scrutiny, this eternity reveals itself as an endless extension of that which formerly fell under the limitation of time.

A large part of the human being is transitory—all of that part which is bound up with the human body and with the objects of sense. But not all of man will pass away. His essential core, his hidden self, his soul, is not subject to time. It is of another nature than the physical body and material objects. It is simple, indestructible, and possessed of mysterious strength. When it forsakes the region of things earthly, it enters the awesome plane where only essences exist, and there it receives a new life, exempt from death, everlasting.

This answer, although looked down upon by those who give the others, is of quite different weight. It corresponds far more closely to our deepest perceptions and more nearly approximates the truth of things. We perceive it, although vaguely, behind the ostensibly scientific and philosophical answers; from it they derive a feeling of security. For what imparts to the positivist, the idealist, and the nobly resigned men such calm conviction—provided it is a conviction to live and die by, and not mere talk and writing—is the hidden hope that, mysteriously, life does go on.

∞

The answer given by religion takes various forms, and is variously fashioned by mythology and metaphysics. Under examination all these interpretations seem to have one thing in common. They abandon the body and equate the immortality of the soul with the conquest of death. In remote antiquity this apparently was not yet the case, and the word we translate as "soul" really meant a sort of double of the whole human being, of his body, his possessions, and his worldly position; it was the mysterious other side of existence. This notion changed in time and came, fairly soon, to mean the immaterial soul in distinction from the body. This is the soul that withstands death, and is of eternal significance.

This is not how Christianity thinks. Modern "spiritualized" and "subjectivized" notions have in no way altered its thinking. It is not soul or spirit Christianity is concerned with, but man. The real question about death affects the concrete human being. Is death a necessity "in the nature of things," or an occurrence that is surmountable? To this question the gospel gives the same answer we began with, a disturbing answer that arouses opposition and yet stirs in us a secret hope.

Sin is the source of all death

It is Christian doctrine that human death is neither self-evident nor yet a necessity of nature; rather, death is the result of something that need never have happened, something that could have been avoided. This doctrine is to be found in the two passages cited earlier from Genesis and Romans. The substance of it is that death is not a constituent part of man's nature, but the result of an act. Death belongs not to the natural but to the historical order.

This doctrine presupposes a view of human nature for which natural concepts alone are insufficient. For animal nature they do suffice. Each animal possesses a nature which contains in itself everything essential to the animal's being. In accordance with the laws of this nature, the form of the animal's growth, maturity, decline, and death unfolds in a self-contained whole. It is not thus with man. His existence is not the unfolding and fulfillment of a nature, but the enactment of a history. He encounters an existence external to his own being, makes his choice, takes his risks, acts, and creates. In this encounter his own nature and being asserts itself continuously. Man's nature is as much the effect as the premise of this encounter. The complete man is determined not at the beginning, but at the end. The shape of a man's life is not a growth and unfolding from within, culminating in a return upon itself; its figure, its symbol, is not the self-enclosed circle, but an arch that reaches out toward something that in turn comes to meet it.

This is not, however, in the manner of the animal, which also lives in a reciprocal exchange with its environment. For the animal, this environment is nothing but an extension of its own form; in some instances it can even be said that animal and environment together form a whole. In any case, this whole is predetermined and subject to natural law, whereas man, on the contrary, possesses true initiative. He is master of his own actions and is given, in unparalleled fashion, an open field. He alone meets and confronts life, and continuously fulfills himself in these encounters.

Man's decisive encounter, however, is with God, for God alone is the true reality, the measure of good. Only in this encounter, and in its repercussions on his life, does man grow into that being which his Creator willed him to be.

∞

Man was created, as Scripture teaches, in a state of high perfection. But although perfect, he was in a state of probation. The Garden of Eden is the figure of the perfection; the tree of knowledge, the figure of the probation. The command not to eat of the fruit of the tree would bring to a decision whether man was willing, in an act of obedience and trust, to throw out the span of his life toward God. Had he stood the test—had he in obedience and generosity of faith, oriented his life according to God's command—then death would not have come into his life.

This doctrine is a touchstone for man's attitude toward revelation. Is revelation for him something fuzzy and vague, providing comfort and haphazard ethical inspiration? Or is it the thing that has changed the world? The first words of Jesus' teaching are: "Do penance, for the kingdom of Heaven is at hand."[4] The warning to repent, to be converted, is taken, and rightly so, first in the moral sense. The hearer is to turn away from evil and turn toward the good. He is to give up his own corrupt will, and to be obedient to God's holy will.

But this is only the beginning of conversion. From this point of view the change should reach out until it takes over the whole life, including the mental life. Man's mind also must be converted, his thinking reconstituted. Let a man recognize that his vision of the world and of himself is the work of his own self-will. Let him look on Revelation for what it is: in it, God, who is greater than the world, who alone is real being, confronts man and summons him to an association that transcends anything that could come to him from himself or from the world. The acknowledgment and acceptance of God's summons is faith.

Thenceforth the man has a new vision; and to acquire the habit of living in the new vision is intellectual conversion. The new vision of the world includes a new vision of man.

[4]Matt. 4:17.

Man is no longer part of animate nature like all the rest, rooted and enclosed in his own nature. His life is proper only to himself. Its movement, its growth, are directed from man to God and back from God to man. And since the higher the position, the greater the risk, it follows that this human existence of ours is at every moment and fundamentally in jeopardy.

∞

Man failed to stand the test. He did not will to span his arch over to the side of God. He willed to be "as God."[5] He willed, that is, to live out from himself, and back to himself. As a result the arch broke, and the term of the break was death.

Even had man not sinned, his life would have come to an end, since life belongs to time. But this end would not have been human death as we know it. We are ignorant of the form it would have taken, since that form never became actuality. All we can say is that there would have been an end which was at the same time a beginning, a passage, and a transformation.

The sin of the first man, with the loss of the great potentiality of his nature, determined the fate of all men. There is in this no injustice, as individualism supposes. We understand it better in these days, now that we are beginning to feel more deeply the close connection between the individual and society. The first man was not the first cipher in a

[5]Gen. 3:5.

numerical series. He was the progenitor of the race. He bore the race in himself, and his decision determined its destiny. Man's history began with his act. It proceeds under sentence of sin and death. As Paul says, "By one man sin entered into this world, and by sin death; so also death passed upon all men in whom [in that first man] all have sinned."[6]

[6]Rom. 5:12.

Death has been made
the bridge to salvation

Death came into the world through sin. This is the answer
Christianity makes to the question of death. It is a bold answer,
which troubles the mind and stirs up opposition. To accept it
requires a mental conversion. But having accepted it, the
mind finds fresh light in nature itself. Revelation, which
comes of God, must be received in faith. Then it lights up
the world about us. Experiences never quite understood, cog-
nitions not borne out by natural knowledge, now make sense.
The modern mind, hearing that death need not necessarily
exist, is either astonished or derisive. But this is only the first
response. Once the instinct for truth is awakened, one
acknowledges that one has felt something of the sort oneself.

Man's natural attitude toward death is one of protest. Besides his sense of self-preservation, which he shares with the
other animals, he has a mental objection. He can see no
sense in death. It is a fact he finds hard to swallow. Not that
he cherishes illusions about biological or other necessary
facts. It is simply that he finds a state of things which admits

death to be not well-ordered. It is not that he is a coward, or not ready, if he ought to, to lay down his life. He may be a brave man, willing to make sacrifices, including life, if need be. Still, against death in itself he must enter his protest.

One hears, or reads, that death has been met willingly, with full consent, by men who accepted it either calmly or in a state of spiritual exaltation. Anyone acquainted with life or death must refuse to believe it. There are, of course, calm and composed deaths, courageous, peaceful, and exalted deaths. To meet death well is one of the highest obligations laid upon human nature. To sacrifice life for a cause or for someone dear to us calls out all that is noble in us. But this is not the point here. It is whether with clear insight and responsible judgment we can affirm that death is in itself an end and purpose acceptable to reason. And that we cannot do. Bread we understand, and light and truth and love we understand. But death, human death, does not make sense.

The Christian religion is certain that death in itself and as such (not "the end") has no proper meaning, and justifies the protest against it. But it also recognizes death as a real thing and acknowledges all its harshness. It rejects any attempt to cover up the bitter reality. Death has its origin not in an inner necessity of human existence, but in sin, the sin of all men, which is also the sin of each individual. To die aright means to recognize this fact and to pay one's account in full.

∞

That is the first point. But Christianity knows something further. In the chapter of Romans from which we have already quoted, Paul says: "If, because of one man's trespass, death reigned through that one man, much more will those who receive the abundance of grace and the free gift of righteousness reign in life through the one man Jesus Christ. Then as one man's trespass led to condemnation for all men, so one man's act of righteousness leads to acquittal and life for all men. For as by one man's disobedience, many were made sinners, so by one man's obedience, many will be made righteous."[7]

When Christ died, something happened to death. Christ died a more real and bitter death than any other man, for death is more deeply death as the life it puts an end to is more greatly life. Christ died as no other man because He lived with an awareness and intensity unequalled by any mere man. This is one truth.

Another truth is that whenever Jesus speaks of His death, He adds that He will rise again. So of the last journey to Jerusalem we read, "From that time, Jesus began to show to His disciples that He must go to Jerusalem, and suffer many things from the ancients and scribes and chief priests, and be put to death, and the third day rise again."[8] Of the death that necessarily results from sin, and exists only as a consequence of sin, there is nothing in the consciousness of Jesus. His death was the step by which His life passed from time into eternity. It was not His soul only that lived on, but His whole human nature, for after He died, He rose to a new life.

[7]Rom. 5:17-19.
[8]Matt. 16:21.

Eternal Life

∞

The word *resurrection* is as strange to modern feeling as the idea that death is not necessary. We still use it as an inheritance from the age of faith, but in a different sense. In contemporary language, it signifies the return of life in spring after the torpor of winter, or some new accession of energy in a man after a period of stagnation. *Resurrection* has come to mean an impulse in the rhythm of life, a rise after a preceding descent. There is nothing of this in the Resurrection of Christ, and through Him of redeemed mankind. It has another, a more exact, a revolutionary meaning.

It means that Christ, after His death, raised Himself up by the sovereign power of the living God to a new and truly human life. It does not mean merely that His soul was immortal and received divine glory in eternity; or merely that His image and His gospel attained a life-giving power in the hearts of those who believed in Him. But it means that His body, after it had died, lived on in a higher way; that His soul, by the power of the Holy Spirit, penetrated and transformed His body; that He entered upon eternal glory in the fullness of His divine and human nature.

This doctrine is not a legendary apotheosis, not a later, mythical structure put on a purely human life, but is found everywhere in the original sources. Christ's Resurrection is as essential a part of the gospel, throughout, as His redeeming death is. The fact that He rose is as much a fact as that He lived at all. Paul leaves us in no doubt: "And if Christ be not risen again, then is our preaching vain. . . . If Christ be not risen [and through Him we ourselves] . . . if in this life only, we have hope in Christ, we are of all men most miserable."[9] Without the Resurrection of Christ, there is no Christianity. Without the Resurrection, Christianity would become something apt to make anyone capable of serious and profound reasoning "of all men the most miserable."

With the death and Resurrection of Christ something happened to death. It ceased to be the mere executing of God's justice, the bitter end with only the "indestructibility of the soul" beyond it. Christ's death has given it a new character, which does not change its form, but does alter its meaning and restore it to what it should have been for the first man— the passage into a new, eternally human life.

The death of Christ, suffered for our sakes, is a fact, and together with His Incarnation and Resurrection, it is simply *the* fact, whether the world wishes it or not. In this fact, which changes everything radically, a man may believe and, by believing, share in it. This participation is man's redemption. Paul cries out, "O death, where is thy victory? O death, where is thy sting?"[10] The "sting" is the hallmark of a death that is the result of sin only, and merely an ending. This mark has been removed, objectively, and for all men, and may be removed for each individual when he enters the community of faith with Christ.

In the same letter, Paul says, "But now Christ is risen from the dead, the firstfruits of them that sleep. For by a man came death, and by a man the resurrection of the dead. And as in Adam all die, so also in Christ all shall be made

[9]1 Cor. 15:14-19.
[10]1 Cor. 15:55.

alive."[11] And again in Romans: "Know you not that all we who are baptized in Christ Jesus are baptized into His death? . . . that as Christ is risen from the dead . . . so we also may walk in newness of life."[12] This "newness of life" is here and now, insofar as the new life, which embraces both body and soul, has been awakened in us by faith and Baptism, and one day will be awakened openly and fully, when it emerges victorious in the glory of the resurrection.

The Resurrection has brought about a fundamental change. No magical cure for death has been found, no new ethical code of dying achieved, which would mean only an advance in the human condition. Death remains a reality. But it has been taken up into a new connection with life and has become the passage into a new life—a divine but eternally human life. For now, beyond our death, awaits the resurrection.

[11]1 Cor. 15:20-22.
[12]Rom. 6:3-4.

Death brings us into
full communion with God

What is death as the Christian sees it?

The man who dies experiences the last consequences of sin. He accepts full responsibility for an act of man, and subjects himself to truth and to the judgment—but not in blank despair. He accepts death as the provision of the living God for his redemption. Death is no longer the dark fear which is the final working out of sin. It has become the means by which man shares in the change wrought by God's great compassion, the change of end into beginning. Death is the entrance into the new life.

The arch we spoke of appears again here. Christ carries man's nature to God and back again from God to man. Rather, not again, but in a new and awesome manner, in the manner of the Incarnation of the Son of God. In this manner we share by faith, not by right of our own nature and being; our share in the Incarnation is owing to grace. Indeed, as Paul repeatedly says, Christian life is the life of Christ in man and of man in Christ. In Christ the arch reaches out to the side of God for each of us. Death is the darkness which the arch has to span.

∞

The new life man attains after death is not merely the extension of the life of the soul, on the premise that the soul, being spiritual, is indestructible. That would be death as Plato conceived it—the soul's emancipation from the limitations and burdens of the body, and its passage into the liberty of a purely spiritual state. What Christ has won for us and proclaims to us is not this. It is something of divine greatness and yet intimately familiar to our inmost nature. It is the deliverance not of the soul only, but of the whole man. It is the remaking of man by God's creative power. Death guarantees the gravity of this deliverance and of this re-creation, for without death the message of the gospel would be sheer fantasy. By His death, Christ anchored the new life in the reality of being; by our death, we legitimately enter into the new life.

The new life that will now be ours after death is not the prolongation of earthly life into the world to come. It is not just the fulfillment of the original urge to live; that would make of death merely a transition from one form of life into another, through some power of transformation inherent in our nature—comparable to the butterfly emerging from a chrysalis. What Christ accomplished and proclaimed was not a matter of natural necessity, but of grace. The new life is the gift of God's free creative power. It is at the same time man's fulfillment; for man's mystery is this: that his life, in the last analysis, is not under an inexorable law, but results from his encounter with God and with His loving freedom. Death is the stern barrier that separates this loving freedom from any noncommittal attitude. Christ's death shows that God is in earnest; ours, that man, who has come into God's love, is in earnest.

The new life that is to come after death is founded in personal relationship with Christ. The difference between now and the hereafter is difficult to express. Ideas and words have to take on a new meaning. The world beyond death is not a transfiguration of this world; it is not simply a deeper understanding of the divine purpose, a revelation and communication of the divine depths, or any such thing; it lies wholly in the person of Christ. Eternal life is a function of His life, into which He entered by His death. His love for us, His invitation to love Him, makes eternal life possible. His gift to us of communion in His love bestows and maintains it. Out of the love that actuated the Redemption, He took our destiny upon Himself, and out of that same love, He makes us sharers in His own destiny. In the mystery of faith and rebirth, we share to the full the life, death, and Resurrection of Christ.

Death is our last venture, with Christ at hand, toward that great promise. In the anguish, dissolution, helplessness, and torturing pain that death may bring, Christ's death is contained. This, however, is only one side—the side turned toward us—of a single whole, of which the other side is the resurrection.

How God purifies
us after death

God purifies us after death

With death the time for willing and acting is over. The life that has been lived now contains the final decision, and the action and accomplishment that issued from it. Man steps out of the enclosure of earthly life into the presence of God and undergoes His judgment.

God is good; He is goodness itself. Goodness is not a measuring rod applicable to everything, including God Himself: it is but another name for God Himself. When the rich young man came to Jesus and addressed Him as "good Master," Jesus answered, "Why callest thou me good? None is good but one: that is God."[13] Goodness is simply God Himself, and the command to be good is His loving will. This will addresses itself to us and requires us to fulfill it.

Inarticulate nature fulfills God's will, but from necessity, for here God's will is expressed in the laws to which nature is subject. To the extent that man is part of nature, he, too, acts

[13]Mark 10:18.

under necessity. But beyond this, man is also a person, and as such God's will addresses him, requiring that it be fulfilled freely. He is not forced to do the holy will. That will, however, is the highest law; and yet room is left for choice: it obliges, but does not compel. In this world God's good will is in a singular position. It is the highest and holiest thing, the all in all, and on its fulfillment hinges the whole meaning of the world. God wills that it should be done, and He wills it with all the intensity of His eternal nature, and He is almighty. Nevertheless He cannot enforce the doing of His will, since it can only be accomplished freely. Consequently the Lord of the world, in the sphere of history, is mysteriously weak. He can only command, require, admonish, and lovingly urge that man, whose salvation depends upon it, recognize the truth and obey it; beyond that He "must" leave room for freedom.

It will be different after death. The closed sphere of history will be opened. The chance to say yes or no will be gone. Happenings and actions have come to an end. Now God confronts man in His holy essence. Sovereign Goodness is one with irresistible power. God wills with divine intensity that good be realized. The look He casts on man becomes the judgment, a judgment that determines man's true being and the shape of his eternal destiny. All this is meant by the words "God judges."

∞

The sentence imposed by this tribunal is final, for it is the truth. In the last analysis, it takes only two forms: acceptance or rejection.

God purifies us after death

People in earlier times had no difficulty understanding this, since they could still distinguish between that which is fundamentally serious and that which is not. But it sounds strange and harsh to modern man. He is used to taking this world seriously; in things earthly he expects the strictest standards to be applied. For that very reason, eternity and eternal destiny have for him lost their gravity. They have been pushed back into the shadowy region of his mind which he likes to think of as "reverence," but whose real name is "indifference" or "cowardice." To get a sudden view of what modern man takes seriously, and what he does not, gives one a feeling of helplessness. It often seems as though the more nearly things approach the center of reality, the lighter they weigh with him. Revelation teaches that these fragmentary lives of ours are of absolute significance, and what we do on earth decides what shall become of us eternally. This is expressed in the doctrine that the sentence of the Last Judgment imposes either redemption or perdition.

∞

Is this all there is to be said about what follows after death? If the life of man were a simple equation of good and evil, it would be all. But human life is not as simple as that. Each man is an extensive, deep-reaching world, in which good and evil exist side by side. He travels a long road, along which right and wrong alternate with each other.

This good and evil, this right and wrong, cannot be clearly separated; they intertwine at every point down to the deepest roots. They do not belong to separate times and occasions;

rather, the present contains the past and lives on in the future. Nor is the good perfectly and fully accomplished. We make an effort, nearly attain the goal, and fall short of it; we struggle, gain ground, lose it, and start all over again. Our actions are wavering and inconsistent. How can we be subjected to an eternal yes or no? God is absolute, but He is also just, and His justice is not exercised upon principles, but upon the life of human beings. There would be an offense to God's truth if some hidden evil were allowed to slip by, and also if some undeveloped or imperfect goodness were denied recognition. The awesomeness of God's judgment is precisely that it truly executes justice. But what does this mean when a final sentence places the chaotic human life under a strict either-or?

The Church teaches that while God's judgment is final in its fundamental decision, still the chance to be cleansed is given to the chaotic and fragmentary human existence. Time, as it were, will be extended into eternity long enough for true justice to be satisfied. The man whose good intention God accepts, but whose life as a whole is not free from evil, will, by purging, be brought to a state which fits him for eternal life. The Church rests this teaching upon certain passages from Scripture: for instance upon the place in the second book of Maccabees where intercession and sacrifices are offered that those who have fallen in battle may be delivered from their sins;[14] upon the words of Jesus about forgiveness in this world and the world to come,[15] and His parable about

---

[14]2 Macc. 12:43-46.
[15]Matt. 12:32.

the debtors' prison from which there is no release until all has been paid;[16] and upon the passage in the first letter to the Corinthians which says that the man who imposed poor materials on the foundation (laid by Christ) would reach eternal life, as it were, by fire.[17] But the main root of the Church's doctrine lies in what is evident from the Christian economy itself. Because God is such as He has revealed Himself to be, and man is what daily experience shows him to be, it is plain that the confusion in human nature must be taken into account.

The belief in purification after death found expression very early in the devotional life of the Church. Commemorations were made for the dead in holy Mass and prayers offered that God might receive them into communion with Him. These prayers and other expressions of concern for the departed presupposed that, although the dead had been accepted by the Divine Judge, they yet remained in an intermediate state.

[16]Matt. 18:34.
[17]1 Cor. 3:11-15.

Our innermost will
determines who we are

Let us take up again from another point of view the line of thought we were following in the previous section.

It is the promise of revealed religion that redeemed man should enter into communion with God. By his encounter with Christ, by grace, and by faith, the new life has been born in him. While time lasts it is a hidden life; at the moment of death it breaks through. From the beginning it was eternal life, since it came from God. In death it becomes eternal in the actual sense of being set free from time, of existing wholly in the present.

But nothing evil can approach God. He is the Holy One. He is purity, righteousness, and the source of every good. He also hates and rejects what is evil, corrupt, or base.

How, then, may a man participate in this new and holy life?

He has seen through the confidence of the so-called "decent," "efficient," "happy to be alive" people and learned in the school of the Faith that this confidence is as superficial as it is noisy, as shallow as it is presumptuous. He has had the courage to face himself as he really is, and to penetrate through the surface to the hidden depths below. He has learned to examine not only his acts, but also his motives, and to pursue his motives down to their hidden roots. Laborious victories and painful defeats, his frequent accountings before God, and the quiet, unceasing admonition within, have destroyed for him the illusions under which "good," "worthy" people hide from themselves the truth. He has reached the point where he sets aside the superficial assurance that "surely everything will turn out right in the end." He feels how impossible it is for someone like him to attain to God.

No doubt the Faith tells us that it is not by himself, but by God's grace,[18] that a man reaches God. Christ's Redemption is His holy pledge. Forgiveness, that act of God exercised not upon what was good, but precisely upon what was bad, in us—that act which springs from the overmastering love of a God who has Himself turned to us to give us absolution—is what raises us to a new life. Man's justification—his being made new—rests upon God, upon what God has planned for him.

True, yet this forgiveness and justification are conceived not as an act of magic, but as a process of reality. Justification is not meant to be merely imputed to man, but should be truly possessed by him. It is not meant to cloak him as an outside garment, but to become one with his innermost will and being.

[18]Cf. Eph. 2:4-8.

Our innermost will determines who we are

So the question assumes another form. Has this justification become so entirely his own and has his life been so thoroughly renewed by grace that he is ready for the full and eternal communion with God?

∞

What, in the last analysis, determines whether a man is good or bad is his inner disposition, his intention. The source of this intention is free will. Man possesses a mysterious mobility of will which enables him, on his own initiative, to strike out in a spiritual direction. By *intention* we mean precisely this inner direction, this underlying purpose, or, rather, the directing will itself, which is possible through freedom; the purpose which is at the beginning of what we call freedom, and which may choose either good or evil, either growth from God or from the self, direction toward God or away from Him.

If his intention is good, man belongs to God. Just as true—even more true, although it is a "hard saying"[19]—is the proposition that if he belongs to God his inner disposition is good.

This is what the angels proclaimed in their *Gloria* over Bethlehem, "Peace to men of good will."[20] "Good will" means grace, and to those who possess it, peace is given. But it also means good intention, and so the *Gloria* is addressed to those whose will is directed toward God, and who therefore are

[19]John 6:60 (Revised Standard Version: John 6:61).
[20]Luke 2:14.

41

pleasing to Him. Thus the two meanings are mysteriously and inseparably one.[21]

But how does this intention manifest itself in actual life? How does this power of initiative which determines the value of our acts present itself? One of its forms, which we can grasp immediately, is what we know as our intention. This we are able to judge and to account for. But this is not all.

Let us suppose that we change our intention; for instance, when, for some reason, it becomes clear that something is out of joint in our life. We examine ourselves, repudiate the wrong committed, and decide in favor of the good, but with the uneasy feeling that we shall slide back into wrongdoing. Insofar as we have control of it, our intention is good. But underneath we may be aware of reservations which, at the moment, we are unable to cope with, but for which we feel responsible.

The complete structure of the thing we call "inner disposition" or intention is composed of various levels, and the moral task consists in penetrating to the deeper resistances with our mastering and ordering efforts. The inner disposition, with all its ramifications, is not easily surveyable and

[21]This applies to all that follows. We shall not hereafter draw particular attention to the truth here laid down. While whatever fits men for the kingdom of God is the work of grace, it is also man's own act, precisely because it is under the action of grace. It is his act as he stands strictly in his own personality before God. We shall consider the whole process of what we call "justification," "sanctification," and "the new life" as it takes place in a living, human mind. What happens, from the human point of view, when man becomes good and fulfills God's commandment to be perfect? What must a man do in good earnest to become perfect?

governable. Some of its levels are withdrawn to the depths of our half-conscious or unconscious life.

Who therefore would dare to claim that his inner disposition is wholly good? The goodness we can answer for reaches as far as we are conscious; what lies beyond is unknown to us. Our effort, our struggle, is to carry this goodness increasingly inward—but what a task it is to make the will good to its very depth!

When a man dies and comes before God, how will it then be with his inner disposition? Suppose a man had started out on a wrong course, with no thought of God, and then later— perhaps very much later—converted. God had touched his heart, and he had done that over which—as the Scriptures tell us—the angels rejoice. In the region of conscious freedom, where he could control it, he had changed his intention and made it good. But how about the depths beneath? The same applies equally to each of us and to "the ninety-nine just men who have no need of repentance."[22] It applies equally to the man who continuously falls, but without ever relinquishing his innermost will to good, and to the man who by constant exertion and self-discipline makes visible progress.

[22]Luke 15:7.

Our intention forms our character and action

Man is called upon to be good; in the Sermon on the Mount he is even exhorted to be "perfect."[23] This means that he has to have the right intention at his crucial point of departure, where freedom begins, and to will the good according to the will of God.

But the command includes more than good intention. To intend the good, to decide in favor of the good, is only the beginning. Intention must be followed by doing and being. It must penetrate from that intimate part of us where, with such mysterious ease, we are in control, into the chaotic, resistant space of things and pressures, the world of action and encounter, of being and growing and self-fulfillment.

To exemplify: I am called upon not only to decide for truth, but to speak the truth. Let us consider what is implied in the speaking of truth. First, my verbal statement has to be correct. That in itself is quite a task; for the tongue slips very

[23]Matt. 5:48.

readily into untruths and half-truths. Then, although the verbal meaning may be accurate, it may be presented in such a way that the listener, without noticing it, is misled. Our will to truth, therefore, should consider that the listener ought to be able to follow us with the same confidence with which the traveler follows a well-built and well-directed road. Again, the words may be wholly true as far as the listener is concerned, yet the speaker may manipulate them for self-deception—for instance, in order to keep a growing inner perception from entering his consciousness, or in order to cover up some inner untruth. The will to truth, therefore, has to penetrate even more deeply and to create order in successive stages.

To turn the intention to tell the truth into the *act* of telling it requires penetration from an upper, easily surveyed layer into ever-deeper depths. Truthfulness would only be achieved once all vital energies are wholly at the disposal of our intention, and truth takes possession of our deepest impulses, voluntary and involuntary, those in view and those out of sight, those half or partly known and those below the conscious level; and even then we have to press on into that contradictory, rebellious, sorry region of our human mind into which we cannot see directly. Who is bold enough to say he is truthful? And when we die, how shall we appear in God's eyes?

∞

We must go further yet. We are commanded not only to *do* good, but to *be* good. Our obligation is to become good, to grow in goodness. Whatever we are or have is the raw material for this growth in goodness—our body and soul, our will, our heart and understanding, our character, our potentialities, our strength and weakness, our personality, our relations with others, our belongings, and our environment.

Just as the intention passes into action, so must the action, in turn, pass into an attitude of the mind until every separate action grows from this attitude. This mental attitude has to become the inner form of the human being, molding his whole character, so that moral obligations acquire the grace and ease of the spontaneous, natural action. What is demanded is the final fusion which makes the good man into the perfect man—perfect as "the Father in Heaven is perfect."[24]

The material furnished for us to work on is, however, worse than formless. It is resistant, rebellious, in large part corrupt and chaotic. The intention must penetrate it through and through. As direction it must introduce order; as goodness it must leaven the whole; as purpose it must find expression in everything. If we examine ourselves with this in mind, we perceive what a thin upper surface our intention has affected; what lies beneath is like soil as yet untouched by the plow.

It is hard work to become good. What labor to become a saint! A saint is one whose whole being has been stirred, in whom the light of God has penetrated the darkness, layer by layer, and transformed it all. How is it with us? How shall we appear before God?

[24]Cf. Matt. 5:48.

∞

And we have not yet reached the end. In its full meaning, being good is an endless process. We believe we are under God's Providence. Each day brings us the tasks that God has assigned to us. Toil, work, effort, self-conquest, sacrifice, and heavy unceasing demands are made upon us, and we know how rarely we fulfill them adequately. To be really good would mean perfectly to achieve what every hour demands, so that life might rise to the full accomplishment of what God has asked of us. What has been left undone can never be recalled, for each hour comes but once, and the next brings its own demands. What is to be done about these gaps and omissions in a life that is so fleeting?

What, also, of the actual wrongdoing? We can gain insight into it and try to do better; but what is done is done and continues to exist. What will be done about that?

We are purified by
facing our sins after death

What happens to the man who at death steps from the closed
sphere of history out into the presence of God, into the light
of His truth that reveals everything, into the power of His
holiness that repels all unholiness?

The Faith teaches that a man pleasing to God—that is, a
man who has been acted upon by grace and animated by
good will—will be accepted by God. The Father's love bestows on him a share in the righteousness of Christ, not
through his own effort, or as a right, but through grace.

This bestowal, however, does not mean that righteousness
is given to man like a cloak to cover the evil and the ugliness
beneath.

But, it will be said, God does forgive sin.

Yes, but again: What does *forgiveness* mean? Is it the same
as the forgiveness with which we forgive each other injuries?
Such forgiveness does not make any real change in the man
who is forgiven. It says no more than, "I have nothing now
against you." God's forgiveness must mean much more. Some

change must take place within the man. Forgiveness cannot mean that the man remains a sinner but God no longer holds it against him. It is something more than a change in God's attitude, leaving the man as he was. The man himself must be so changed by it that he becomes "well pleasing" to God.

But, it will be answered, God's love remakes the man.

It does, indeed, ultimately, but let us proceed here with caution, for although God is almighty, He is not a magician. God's love fashions anew, but fashions in reality; He gives a "new heart" and a "new life."[25] But what has been done has not been undone. Here is a gap that has to be filled. There must be change, purification, and reparation. This is the point to which we have been moving.

A man who has died has left time behind. The "day" has gone in which he can "do the works of God."[26] Now there is no more for him to do; all that remains is to be. Is there no further change then?

No further change will affect the man who has crossed over from time to eternity in the state of perfection. Justified by God's judgment, he stands in the pure present of eternal life.

Nor does further change affect the man whose will was evil up to the end. He has been rejected by God, and is immutably fixed in the lost state of everlasting death.

But what about the man whose will was good, although not sufficiently good to extend to his whole being, the man whose intention has not penetrated sufficiently below the

[25]Cf. Ezek. 36:26; Rom. 6:4.
[26]John 9:4.

surface to reach the settled resistance beneath and the depths filled with evil and impurity, the man whose whole life is rid-dled with omissions and bears in itself the ravages of wrong-doing?

It may be argued that this is too human an approach; that when a man comes before God, the things of earth and time no longer matter. In the presence of what alone is important—the holy power, the love, and the grace of God—what does it matter whether in our fragmentary and confused existence we have sinned either by omission or by action and error, whether we are still harboring weaknesses, deficiencies, inconsistencies, or blind spots? If the one thing necessary—the union of grace and freedom in God's good pleasure—is present, then from this source, all things are present and from it arises "the liberty of the children of God,"[27] as the absolute creation of God's power of love.

So great and devout a thought seems utterly convincing; yet it is not correct. A great thought may be deceptive if it fails to take account of small things when they, too, are true. Redemption is not a work of enthusiasm. It is a work of love, and of love that is truth. God's grace brings about everything, but not by a method that simply cancels all that was done on earth, the weaknesses in the structure of our life, the faults, and the blindness. They are still there, in God's sight, since He is truth. His work of love is not to wipe out the earthly deficiencies, but to bring them all under the action of truth, and to consume them, one by one, down to the smallest, in their entirety, down to their roots.

[27]Rom. 8:21.

But how is this to be done once time is past and man can do no more? He can do one more thing, says the Church—he can suffer. His suffering is both the outcome of his condition and its cure.

When such a man enters into God's light, he sees himself as God sees him. He loves God's holiness, and hates himself because he contravenes it. He feels his condition fully. What he has been, what he may have vaguely guessed about himself, he now experiences clearly. He experiences himself as the thing he is in God's sight. The pain of this realization is inconceivable, but it is effective. In this pain man's disposition is purified and expanded until it reaches its full measure of good will. It penetrates into the vital forces of man's being with a cleansing fire, until he attains the state of readiness for communion with God. It acts upon man's being until he not only desires the good, but has made goodness itself his own form. In this process of becoming, dying and living again are bound up in an astounding, terrifying mystery. Death upon death has to be endured so that new life may arise.

The process extends even to the gaps, the omissions. These are not reconstituted as if by a magic trick. In the surrender of the creature to the re-creating will of God, however, his negligences are repaired. Otherwise, there would always remain the dregs of resignation and despair. The pain that was refused must be accepted; the truth that has escaped cognition must be learned; the imperfect love must be made full and perfect. The past is not substituted for, since there is no substitute for a unique event.

We are given some hints as to the mystery of man's restoration, most of all in our understanding of contrition. True contrition is not merely sorrow over our failures, for that would but emphasize the gaps. It is not merely the resolve to do better next time, which leaves the past as it was. The contrite man returns to the past act and enters into it until he knows and judges it with his reason, his will, and his intention, and does so in the presence of the living, holy God. Contrition is more than facing the past act. The past act is frankly defined and taken up into the beginning of the new creation, the creation wrought by the power of the Holy Spirit, and the act is by Him formed anew. Psychology gives us another intimation. A demand made in early youth, or at some other vulnerable period, if refused, may fasten and fester below the level of consciousness, in the unconscious, and from there exercise a destructive effect upon the entire life. And there is no remedy except to reconstruct the wrong action. The person must bring the whole action back into consciousness, face what he did amiss, make amends where possible, and so restore his life to order.

These are slight intimations, nothing more, not proofs or examples. We have to do with the mystery of a grace that forgives and creates anew. When he is judged, the man sees himself entirely in the holy light of God; sees the circumstances, the causes, the accidental and the essential; sees the outside and the inside; sees to the very bottom, what was known to him or what was hidden from him because it lay too deep, or had been forgotten, suppressed, or slighted. And he sees it all without a shadow of protection. Pride, vanity, evasion, and indifference are gone. He is exposed, sensitive, and collected. He is on the side of truth in opposition to himself. He is prepared to face his own life with its undone duties, its loose ends, its muddle. In a mystery of suffering, the heart adjusts itself to contrition and delivers itself up to the power of the holy Creator-Spirit. Opportunities misused are rebestowed, wrong turns retraced and taken rightly. Evil, by being lived again, is made over into good. The improvement is not an external matter. The whole nature, plunged into re-creating grace, through the mystery of effectual repentance, comes out newly made.

The Church calls this Purgatory.[28] Let no rightly disposed heart say it is no concern of his. Rather does not what is deepest in us respond thankfully to the assurance that it shall be thus? Does it not say, "I wish I had reached that goal"?[29]

---

[28]Once more, what has been said does not cover the whole subject. No mention has been made of expiation, which is part of purifying suffering and a point which may help clarify its meaning.

[29]From the point of view here set forth it will be seen in how many ways our concept of the departed has become distorted. The expression "poor souls," although devout and charged with loving solicitude, contains much that is petty and belittling. The dead in the hand of God do not, as such, call for pity. They are undergoing inconceivable suffering, but suffering that is of value. If a person we love very much had taken a wrong course, and were one day to see the light, and we were to see him in the distress of conversion, should we pity him? Rather, we should yearn over him, bear his distress with him, knowing always that something tremendous was taking place, and hold it in the deepest reverence. We must, therefore, erase from our ideas about the departed all pettiness, all that may express man's secret desire to see the suffering of another, all busying oneself with "helping" them, and all importunate pleading for mercy. Scripture teaches us otherwise. These are the sons and daughters of God who are undergoing affliction, but, at the same time, are in expectation of their delivery from servitude into "the liberty of the children of God." . . .

We will rise again,
both body and soul

Scripture says the dead will rise again

Some of the questions which occupy the human mind rise out of particular occasions and may be set aside, but there are others which must be faced, or we shall be left helplessly in the dark about the essentials of existence. Among these latter are the questions concerning the "last things." What will happen at the end? Will it be a final fulfillment of life, or does death end all? If death does not end all, what new form will my life take in consideration of all I have done and been through?

The Faith answers that the first among these last things, death, must be faced in sober earnest, accepted, and endured. But death is only one side of a great event; the other side is the resurrection.

∞

Toward the end of the last book in Holy Scripture, the mysterious book of Revelation of the apostle John, we read:

"And I saw a great white throne, and one sitting upon it from whose face the earth and Heaven fled away, and there was no place found for them. And I saw the dead, great and small, standing in the presence of the throne, and the books were opened; and another book was opened which is the book of life; and the dead were judged by those things which were written in the books according to their works. And the sea gave up the dead that were in it, and death and Hell gave up their dead that were in them, and they were judged, every one, according to their works."[30]

∞

In the first letter to the Thessalonians, Paul writes: "For if we believe that Jesus died, and rose again, even so them who have slept through Jesus, will God bring with Him [risen like Himself]. For this we say unto you in the word of the Lord, that we who are alive, who remain unto the coming of the Lord, shall not have any advantage over them who have slept. For the Lord Himself shall come down from Heaven with His commandment, and with the voice of an archangel, and with the trumpet of God: and the dead who are in Christ shall rise first."[31]

And in the first letter to the Corinthians, we read: "For if the dead rise not again, neither is Christ risen again. And if Christ be not risen again, your faith is vain, for you are yet in your sins. They also who are fallen asleep in Christ are

[30]Rev. 20:11-13.
[31]1 Thess. 4:13-15.

perished. If, in this life only, we have hope in Christ, we are of all men most miserable."[32]

These passages only develop what Jesus proclaimed in the gospel. When the Sadducees, who denied the resurrection, asked what would happen in eternity to the woman who had had many husbands, all of whom had died—whose wife would she be?—He replied, "You err, not knowing the Scriptures nor the power of God. For in the resurrection, they shall neither marry nor be married; but shall be like the angels of God in Heaven. And concerning the resurrection of the dead, have you not read that which was spoken by God, saying, 'I am the God of Abraham, and the God of Isaac, and the God of Jacob'? He is not the God of the dead, but of the living."[33] And even if Jesus, in His discourse on the last things[34] does not speak expressly of the resurrection, yet the thought is behind all He says and determines its meaning.

Revelation teaches also that death is not the end, but that man, having died, will rise again to a new life. As Christ's hearers said when they heard the message of the Eucharist: "This saying is hard, and who can hear it?"[35] In this instance, too, there have been attempts to remove the stumbling block. The doctrine of the resurrection, it has been said, is not essential to the message of Jesus, but grows from man's natural urge to live, which refuses to come to terms with death. However, there is no question that the doctrine of resurrection is a fundamental part of the gospel. It was believed

[32]1 Cor. 15:16-19.
[33]Matt. 22:29-32.
[34]Matt. 24 and 25.
[35]John 6:60 (Revised Standard Version: John 6:61).

from the first, it has been held firmly through the centuries, and wherever Christian faith is truly alive, it has withstood all modern efforts to water it down.

Again, the doctrine of the resurrection is said to be the product of the classical feeling for the body, since the ancients were unable to think of life apart from the body. When they were presented with the doctrine of eternal life, they conceived it in bodily terms and consequently made it necessary to speak of it as a resurrection.

Christianity was concerned only with the immortality of the soul and its return to God. This idea is as untenable as the other. In the first place, it is not correct that classical man could conceive of life only in bodily terms. Through the whole intellectual history of Greece runs a current of thought, to which Plato[36] gives powerful expression, that insists that genuine life is possible only to a pure spirit. It is a current which invaded Christianity itself, and as early as the first century, the Church had to struggle against Gnosticism, which rejects everything material. It was a fight which lasted for centuries and by means of which the belief in the resurrection was clarified and deepened. As regards St. Paul, who proclaimed so emphatically the belief in the resurrection of the dead, he was far from deriving it from the classical feeling for the body. The man who said, "Unhappy man that I am: who shall deliver me from the body of this death?"[37] would have been inclined by nature and temperament to find reality in spirit and mind only.

[36]Greek philosopher (427-347 B.C.).
[37]Rom. 7:24.

Had it been a matter of the immortality of the soul only, there would have been no need for a Christian revelation. Pythagoras,[38] Socrates,[39] and Plato had all taught it. It is truly the resurrection of the dead and man's eternal life with which we are concerned. To remove this doctrine from Christian consciousness is not possible.

---

[38]Greek philosopher and mathematician (sixth century B.C.).
[39]Greek philosopher and teacher (470-399 B.C.).

Both body and soul will rise again

One's natural reaction to the doctrine of the resurrection is to be troubled by it. As early as the first letter to the Corinthians, Paul was forced to ask: "If Christ be preached, that He rose from the dead, how do some among you say that there is no resurrection of the dead?"[40] There were people who denied the doctrine then as there have been ever since. There were those who denied it even among those who knew and conversed with Christ, to whom He gave testimony of the doctrine.[41] It was denied in the Middle Ages when Gnosticism had grown so powerful and taken such various forms. It is disclaimed in modern times, and with even greater confidence, since to a modern man the idea that the dead will rise again is hardly thinkable. Natural science makes it certain that there exists in the whole range of experience no force that can restore an organism fallen into decay. Our

[40]1 Cor. 15:12.
[41]Matt. 22:23-33.

strong feeling for life also, which throws itself so unreservedly into the stream of purely earthly existence, makes us accept and will death, since death and birth are admittedly only surface waves on a ceaselessly flowing whole.

But before going further, let us be clear about a fundamental point which was spoken of in the first chapter.

Knowledge has truth as its object, and truth is one and all-inclusive. Truth means that that which is, is understood by the mind in the light of eternal reality. In order to achieve this, the mind must approach the various spheres of reality according to the requirements of each sphere. To find out the truth about animate nature, I may not apply a framework of reference proper to inanimate nature. An intellectual truth requires a different approach from that required by a truth concerning mechanics. Truth is only illuminating if man approaches it in a spirit corresponding to its requirements. The higher the object, the greater the demands upon the mind that would know it—the greater also the temptation to draw it down to lower levels where things are more comfortably managed. It is very enticing to think of the process of life in terms of chemistry, or to deal with the mind in terms of biology. It saves effort and has the advantage of appearing as scientific inquiry. Actually, it is plain mental laziness, which violates the true process of cognition and loses sight of the true nature of the object under investigation.

If all this applies to the natural mental processes in relation to the world which is their object, how much more to Revelation! In Revelation, God, the sovereign Lord of the world, addresses the world; consequently, in Revelation, men are faced with a wholly new reality. It is the hallmark of a genuine revelation that it cannot be deduced from any forms or potentialities of this world, but rather is utterly independent of them and, indeed, disrupts them. Revealed truth can only be recognized if we cease to approach it with earthly standards and are prepared to accept it on its own terms. This is the first and determining approach.

But there is a second. The God of Revelation is also the Creator of the world. When His Word comes into the world, it comes not as to a strange place, but "to His own."[42] And although, indeed, Revelation must be accepted without justification by earthly standards, once accepted, it forthwith throws its light upon this very world, encourages it to ask questions of essential importance to it, and gives answers far exceeding natural wisdom.

If our thinking is to be Christian, and the content of Revelation comprehended for what it really is, our minds must undergo a change. Jesus commands us to be converted.[43] The obligation rests upon the mind as well as upon the will. Real in the natural sense are the things we find about and within us. True in the natural sense are the ideas in which this reality becomes transparent; possible in the natural sense is what is possible to the things in this world. Real in the Christian sense is that which Revelation discloses as real; true in the Christian sense is that which is opened to us by the Word and the Spirit of God; possible in the Christian sense is that which is attested as possible in Christ. These things are easily said, but difficult to live in accordance with.

[42]John 1:11.
[43]Matt. 4:17.

Eternal Life

It does not follow that because a man decides to accept the Faith, he really thinks according to the Faith. If our minds, deeply habituated as they are to ways of thought which, for more than a century, have been drawn more and more deeply into this world, if our minds are fully to possess the content of Revelation, they must undergo a thorough reconstruction. And only in proportion to the extent of this reconstruction shall we understand what Christ says about the resurrection.

∞

In Christianity it is not the spirit that matters, but man. When we first read what the philosophers and religious thinkers say about the immortality of the soul and the eternal life of the spirit, we are moved by its power and inspiration. But when we take it under closer scrutiny, in order to find out how this immortal life is constituted and how it deals with the harvest of our earthly life, all that we call our history—what we do and what befalls us—then the ideas of the philosophers become blurred. To believe in the immortality of the soul apart from the body means that historical reality must be renounced and actual existence dissolved in rhetoric.

What interests the Christian is quite a different matter—namely, how the actual world is to be redeemed, and what is to become, in eternity, of the person and of the events of his life. Christianity is not a metaphysics; it is the witness to Himself of the true God. It is the proclamation that God has seized upon earthly existence and will carry it on to a new state in which the old is not lost, but rather will receive its ultimate meaning. This is all bound up with the body. Strange though it may sound, the final clarification as to what is meant by *the person* and by *personal existence*, by the *fate* of individuals and of mankind, becomes evident in the position assigned to the body. If the body does not rise, then an immortality of the spirit alone becomes, to speak frankly, rather indifferent.

Christianity is not concerned with the idea, the essence of man, but with the reality of man, with his responsibilities and his human dignity, his actions and his destinies—briefly, with his history. History and body, however, are inseparable. The resurrection of the body safeguards man as a personal and historical being and sets him off, on one side, from nature, and on the other, from metaphysics and myth.

Our resurrected bodies will reflect our history

A further point must be made at once. The ground of man's bodily life is Christ. The resurrection is not a further stage in the progress of life, a new form developed after death out of man's own potentialities. It is a response to a summons from the most high God. God willed man to be man. To be man is to be spirit expressed and made active through the body. To be man is to be a bodily organism, subject to the operation of a personal spirit that bestows on that organism a form and capacity which, of itself, it is powerless to attain; to be man is to occupy a specific place in history, in which the spirit, with its dignity and responsibility, takes its stand. Resurrection therefore signifies that the spiritual soul, true to its nature, again becomes the soul of a body—indeed that only now is it fully liberated and empowered to inform the body. Resurrection signifies that the matter from which the soul has departed once more becomes personalized, spiritualized corporeality, that is, a human body although no longer limited by time and space, but which has become, as Paul says, a spiritual, a "pneumatic" body.[44]

We do not know what that body will be like. But from various sayings in the Pauline letters, and also from the book of Revelation, it would seem to be, together with the idea of "a new Heaven" and "a new earth,"[45] the fulfillment of the redeemed world. In the eighth chapter of Romans, Paul, speaking of the essence of the Christian hope, says: "For I reckon that the sufferings of this time are not worthy to be compared with the glory to come that shall be revealed in us. For the expectation of the creature waiteth for the revelation of the sons of God. For the creature was made subject to vanity, not willingly, but by reason of him that made it subject, in hope; because the creature also itself shall be delivered from the servitude of corruption into the liberty of the glory of the children of God. For we know that every creature groaneth and travaileth in pain, even till now. And not only it, but ourselves also, who have received the firstfruits of the Spirit—even we ourselves groan within ourselves, waiting for the adoption of the sons of God, the redemption of our body."[46]

This redemptive perfection is grace, and issues from God's absolute freedom. Therefore it cannot be measured with earthly measures, nor can we deduce its conditions from conditions in this world. Yet it is this world that is to be made perfect by grace, and there are present everywhere in it

[44]1 Cor. 15:44.
[45]Rev. 21:1.
[46]Rom. 8:18-23.

intimations that reveal an affinity with what comes from God. We may therefore ask whether in physical matter (as we call it) there are not indications discernible that point beyond the potentialities of this earth.

A difference in essence is perceptible between a lifeless object and a plant. A crystal possesses concentrated material form that is clear, exact, and precious, but also heavy, hard, and inert. How different appears an apple tree, which pushes out from the ground and, in growing, changes and develops, blossoms and bears fruit—in a word, is alive. It, too, is matter, but of another kind. It has conquered inertia; it lifts up trunk and branches into the sky and develops from its proper core. A new difference shows in the animal. A horse and a bird are as much matter as a stone and a tree, but the horse and bird have the capacity of free movement and of perception and action. They maintain and defend themselves, produce offspring and tend them, and the bird even builds its own habitation.

A further difference appears between man and animal. Whereas animals are confined to certain immutable possibilities and conditions, practically merging with their environment, man possesses creative initiative unlimited in range. He is capable of discerning truth and of making moral decisions. He has a liberty of action and performance that makes it possible for him even to destroy himself through his own daring. These powers give rise to a corporal nature of a new kind. Not only is it more subtle and highly organized than that of the others, but it has qualities that connect it with all living things and endow it with a sort of universality.

In all of these different kinds of existing things, we find "body"—in the crystal, the apple tree, the horse, and the bird, and in the man I am addressing. At each stage physical matter is put at the service of a new principle that gives it not only fresh qualities and capacities, but indeed, at every stage, a new character. Stage by stage it overcomes inertia, weight, bondage, and muteness, and gains lightness, space, height, and freedom; its sphere of operation broadens, and the operations themselves increase in importance. Both the power to act and the scope for action are enlarged. Matter increasingly becomes material for the spirit to work upon. In man, body has universal significance. It is not only the highest stage in bodily development, but corporeity in its very essence.

∞

Does this line of development stop with man as we know him? Our intuitive feeling tells us it must proceed further. Humanity is not a blind alley. The possibilities of what we call "body" are inexhaustible. A clear and direct indication of what they are is furnished by the rising stages the body reaches in man himself. For the human body is not a finished, arrested form; it is ever in process of becoming. That a healthy body kept in condition by care and exercise is more "body" than a neglected one is self-evident. But does the body reach its greatest dignity and perfection in the face and carriage of a man who lives among noble objects and pursues a thinking life, or in the trained and healthy but anti-intellectual and superficial man? If the question surprises us, it is because we are in the habit of looking at the human body much as we look at the animal body: as nature merely. But the human body is definitely determined by spirit.

Our resurrected bodies will reflect our history

The face of a man who is passionately searching for truth is not only more "spiritual" than that of the man with a dulled mind; it is also more of a face, that is to say, it is more genuinely, more intensively "body." And not only is there more "spirituality" in the bearing of a man with a free and generous heart than in that of a crude and selfish person, but also there is a more responsive body. With man begins a wholly new scale of development. The body as such becomes more animated, more vibrating, as it is more strongly informed by the life of the heart, mind, and spirit.

One of the modern dogmas is that the Middle Ages neglected the body. Not only is this idea wrong, but it also proves willful blindness. Anyone not biased by prejudice must perceive the richness of life that is manifested in the faces and figures of medieval art. It signifies that here a new feeling for the body has arisen which gives it a quality beyond that reached in the art of antiquity, and which testifies to a new freedom of the heart. Its origin is in the Christian experience—in the life lived in relation to God and in fellowship with Christ. The body took no damage from the association, as dull conformity maintains, but gained from it fresh energy, depth, and harmony, the effects of which are still noticeable even where the Christian conviction has long been abandoned.

For the body is but partially the work of nature; another— perhaps the more important—part is due to the work of the soul. This part is fashioned by a daring mind, by the renunciations of a valiant heart. Often, deep suffering and even apparent ruin are its fashioning tools. Renunciation and sacrifice, which to the dull eye appear as modes of destruction, to a clearer view appear as changes of form leading to a higher bodily manifestation. Rembrandt, Roger van der Weyden, and Matthias Grünewald could not have painted the magnificently expressive faces and figures of their canvases had not the saints in their striving after God cast their bodies into the furnace of sacrifice.

Let us beware of taking too cheap a view of human life. Nature alone never produced anything great; greatness is the work of self-conquest and sacrifice.

What, then, will not be possible when eternity breaks into time and when divine strength and holiness hold unrestricted sway, setting the spirit free in its absolute purity and power?

The passage on the resurrection in the first letter to the Corinthians refers to this. Paul says: "But some man will say, 'How do the dead rise again? Or with what manner of body shall they come?' Senseless man, that which thou sowest is not quickened except if it die first. And that which thou sowest, thou sowest not the body that shall be, but bare grain, as of wheat. . . . But God giveth it a body as He will: and to every seed its proper body. All flesh is not the same flesh, but one is the flesh of men, another of [four-footed] beasts, another of birds, another of fishes. And there are bodies celestial and bodies terrestrial; but one is the glory of the celestial and another of the terrestrial. One is the glory of the sun, another the glory of the moon, and another the glory of the stars, for star differeth from star in glory. So also is the resurrection of the dead. It [man's body] is sown in corruption; it shall rise in incorruption. It is sown in dishonor; it shall rise in glory. It is sown in weakness; it shall rise in power.

It is sown a natural body; it shall rise a spiritual body. . . . The first man was of the earth, earthly; the second man, from Heaven, heavenly. Therefore, as we have borne the image of the earthly [in us], let us bear also [in ourselves] the image of the heavenly."[47]

Quite apart from its value as Revelation, taken only as reasoning, the passage ranks high. In some points it is not quite clear. As in everything Paul utters, he is overwhelmed by spiritual experience. But the fundamental meaning, the nature of the body, is written large and plain. Paul uses the unscientific language of immediate experience. There is the body of plants, differing from plant to plant; the body of animals which differs again in each species; the body of the stars, which in the thought of antiquity were mysterious, semi-divine beings, every star having a body peculiar to itself. Thus develops an unending series of differing natures and degrees of dignity. It extends beyond the potentialities of this world, beyond the earthly sphere, and over into the spiritual and heavenly.

Between the differing forms of bodies, there is, at times, a sharp cleavage, sometimes so sharp that there is no bridging it. Stones do not become birds. But between other forms, in spite of differences, there is an immediate connection, one phase passing into another without an intermediary, as the seed corn passes into grain. The cleavage between these forms is spanned, by the mystery of germination.

Still, the gap has to be bridged. That requires what Paul calls a "death." The seed, if a new plant is to replace the old,

[47]1 Cor. 15:35-47, 49.

must sink into the ground and die, that is to say, give up its form so that a new plant may come to life. So also is it with man. Man, too, has two forms of body, an earthly and a heavenly, and the earthly is to the heavenly as the seed is to the wheat. Death lies between them. The body must be laid in the earth and decay before the new and heavenly body comes into being. At this point the analogy fails. The plant "grows" directly "from" the seed, from its structure and its functions; but the heavenly body does not grow in the same fashion from the earthly body. The seed, by virtue of the identity of its forms, both being "wheat," through its decay becomes alive in the new plant. The human body, however, after death must be "awakened." The force which raises it does not derive from its inner nature, but from the beyond, from God's free power.

What that power is, is known as the resurrection. It is the power that raised Christ from the tomb. By the same power Christ awakens His own from death and fashions them to a new and heavenly life. But its spiritual and heavenly character, which is the mark of that life, does not denote merely a higher stage in existence, as of animal over plant, or man over animal. It is a wholly new life issuing from God's sovereign power. It is the work of the Holy Spirit, who came into the world at Pentecost and has been its governor and ruler ever since.

At Pentecost began a new line of descent. Earthly man bore the nature of his earthly ancestor Adam. But when Christ, the Heavenly Man, came, He began a new line of descent which takes the form of its nature, the quality of its life, from Him. As the first letter to the Corinthians says: "Now

Our resurrected bodies will reflect our history

Christ is risen from the dead, the firstfruits of them that sleep. For by a man came death, and by a man the resurrection of the dead. And as in Adam all die, so also in Christ all shall be made alive [again]. But every one in his own order: the firstfruits Christ, then they who are of Christ, who have believed in His coming. Afterwards the end, when He shall have delivered up the kingdom to God the Father, and when He shall have brought to nought all principality, and power, and virtue . . . and the enemy death shall be destroyed last."[48]

The same applies to the restoration of man.

But are there not biological objections? Biology, if it sticks to what it really knows and does not, after rejecting the Church's dogmas, set up very questionable dogmas of its own, must acknowledge that it has nothing whatsoever to say on the subject. It cannot on its own premises affirm that a resurrection is possible, and certainly not that it is impossible. And what modern physics has to say of the significance of form in the structure of matter, and what medicine has to say of the influence of the mind upon the body, would indicate that the body is at the disposal of the spirit in a way never before suspected.

∞

We have not yet finished with our thoughts on the risen body. The natural body is not only a fixed, spatial form, but it has also had a history. From its origin to its decay, it goes through an endless number of forms. Which of these is properly

[48]1 Cor. 15:20-26.

its own? Is it the child's, the mature man's, the elderly man's? The answer can only be: all are essential. The individual form does not exist only that the next should take its place, and so on, one after the other, in order that the last one, death, might appear. Each phase is the man, and each is indispensable to his life as a whole. That endless series of configurations which is the human body must be included in the resurrected body. It must have a new dimension, that of time, but time raised to the power of eternity with the result that its history is included in its present, and all the successive moments of its past exist in an absolute now.

Besides man's history, in the sense of successive developments, in the sense of what he has done or what has happened to him, there must be present also his joys, sorrows, frustrations, liberations, victories, defeats, and love, and hatred. All the unending experiences of the soul were expressed in and by the body and have become part of it, contributing either to its development or to its crippling and destruction—all are present and retained in the risen body. The pattern of the life is there with all that befell the man, for the resurrection of the body means the resurrection of the life that has been lived, with all its good and all its evil.

And what are the limits of a man's body? Surely his clothes belong to it since they performed the double function of protection and expression. What of his work tools, the articles he kept about him, his house, and his much-loved garden. What of the whole sphere of his life? Let us not be too fanciful; yet it is certain that the body goes beyond its mere anatomical limits. Fundamentally it is limitless. It is the essence of man's earthly existence in visible form. In the resurrection, form, substance, and life will all rise. Nothing that has been is annihilated. Man's deeds and his destiny are part of him, and, set free from the restrictions of history, will remain for eternity, not by any power of his own, not as a final phase of an inner development, but at the summons of the Lord Almighty, and in the strength of His Spirit.

∞

Man will rise to his salvation, or to his eternal perdition. The body will be blessed or accursed.

But how will it stand with the body of the man in need of purification, of whom we have spoken in the second chapter? If man, after his death, is in need of purification, this is true also of his body. But how shall that body be purified if it rises only at the end of time when blessedness and accursedness are the only alternatives? Although there is no explicit answer, we can at least indicate the direction in which the answer may be found.

Soul and body are not clearly separable entities. The body is continuously informed by the spiritual soul; indeed, what we call body is, at every point, in every act, one with the soul. If the soul could be completely removed, there would be no body, but only a biological substance, perhaps of mutually destructive chemical particles. The soul, on its side, does not live on its own account, but is effective in and through the body, to the point that it seems doubtful whether a single purely spiritual act is possible in human life. Throughout, it is spirit-body that is human. The soul, as we say, is "in" the body, meaning that it is the principle of its life, the content of its appearance, and the purpose behind its activity. But we might as well say that the body is "in" the soul, and mean that the soul embraces the body as its means of operation, as the revelation of its hidden nature, as material for its historical existence, as form and act; for the fate of the body is conferred upon it by the quickening soul.

When at death the soul leaves the body, it does not leave the bodily sphere altogether. It does not become an angel. It remains a *human* soul. As such its bears the body within itself. The soul was the premise of the body and the expression of its life, and that fact is unforgotten. The soul, as the scholastics said, is the body's form, and not a form in general, but the form of a particular body. It is not its blueprint only, but contains its whole experience, not as an agent of the body's activity alone, but also as effecting its own development, taking up bodily happenings into itself. This falls in with the resurrection of the dead, for in the resurrection, God has given the soul with its body-forming power the opportunity to build up the body entrusted to it as it was meant to be.[49]

If this is true, and the soul undergoes the purification we spoke of, then, if we may put it so, the latent body will be equally cleansed, so that when the dead man rises, his new body will have been made fit for a soul purified and made absolute.

---

[49]Dante, the great poet of the hereafter, has extraordinary things to say about the power of the soul to construct the body. It throws considerable light on the true concept of Christianity in this matter when we observe that the greatest Christian poem (*The Divine Comedy*), which also expresses most effectively the very essence of the Middle Ages, is filled with the richest and strongest feeling for the body.

Our resurrected bodies will reflect our history

The making of the new body is no sudden event. It is not as if man were an earthly creature up to his death, and then, at the Lord's Coming, would be thrust at once into a spiritual and heavenly state. Paul, in his letter to the Romans, explains the other side of this doctrine. In the sixth, seventh, and eighth chapters, he shows in powerful developments of thought that the mystery of death and resurrection has already begun in this world: "Know you not that we, who are baptized in Christ Jesus, are baptized in His death? For we are buried together with Him by Baptism into death; that as Christ is risen from the dead [to a new life] by the glory of the Father, so we also may walk in newness of [the same] life. For if we have been planted together in this likeness of His death, we shall be also in the likeness of His Resurrection. Knowing this, that our old man is crucified with Him, that the body of sin may be destroyed, to the end that we may serve sin no longer."[50]

Baptism, as the very beginning of the mystery, is at once death and resurrection. In Baptism the "new man" is born. Thereafter he lives, although cloaked by the old, in the inner core of the believer. From now on, life is a mysterious interchange of becoming and ceasing to be. In all actions, in all happenings, the death of the old man and the resurrection of the new are in continuous process. Dying consists in continuous turning to God, in obedience, self-conquest, renunciation, effort, and struggle, in all that we call the imitation of Christ.[51]

[50]Rom. 6:3-6.
[51]The inspired rhapsody ending chapter eight of Paul's letter to the Romans expresses the new life that arises from such dying.

Christ's Incarnation ensures
our own bodily resurrection

This train of thought may have the most far-reaching consequences. The fact that the importance of the body in Christianity is again perceived and experienced, and is returning
to its central position in the Christian consciousness, may
well indicate a decisive change in the spiritual history of
Christianity.

What this change would imply is not easy to express. The
era since the ending of the Middle Ages seems characterized
by a new trend in human thought: the emergence of a radical
division between brute matter, on the one hand, and pure intellect in the form of reason on the other. The tension between these two poles had led to tremendous accomplishments.
Modern science and technology are its products. But another
result has been the loss, to a large extent, of the concept of
body informed by the soul, of spirit embodied as tangible reality. Actually, man himself has been lost, and with man,
the things themselves. In the great achievements of our age,
this has long remained unnoticed, although gradually we are

becoming aware of our loss. We are now experiencing its consequences, if only in the form of a feeling of emptiness and nostalgia.

Christianity also suffered from the division. Although it is true that in its essence it is above the shifting currents of history, and is safeguarded by faith, obedience, and love, yet its modes of interpretation are subject to historical change. As a consequence, Christian life has been separated into spiritual abstraction on the one hand, and, on the other, into material and organizational concerns; man, as form imbued with spirit, as image and symbol, lost much of his vitality in this process.

A change, however, seems now to be setting in. We are recognizing that the peculiar bent of the Christian consciousness is not toward God in Himself, but toward God incarnate in man, Jesus Christ. Our interest is not in the salvation of the spirit or soul, but in the living creature, man, and in the salvation of the world through man. It is the "new man"[52] and the "new Heaven" and the "new earth"[53] that interest us.[54]

What it was that God set out to do; what is meant by His becoming Man, and after the death and Resurrection of Christ

[52]Eph. 4:24.

[53]Rev. 21:1.

[54]Here a brief comment. The frequently quoted words of Mark 8:36 are usually translated, "For what shall it profit a man, if he gain the whole world and suffer the loss of his soul?" A better rendering would be "suffer the loss of his life." For the Greek *psyche* signifies soul as the life principle, but not as separable from the life. And while it is unnecessary here to go into philosophical niceties, it is well to establish the fact that Jesus was no spiritualist. His concern is not for the "soul," but for the man. Concern for the soul alone brought about the Gnosticism of the ancients and the spiritualism of our own time.

by remaining Man; what is meant by the Manhood of Christ being placed for all eternity at the right hand of the Father on the throne of everlasting glory—as to all this it would be well for us to clarify our ideas. Who is God, if these things are true—indeed the truth, the redeeming, sanctifying, life-giving truth? Not, certainly, the Absolute Spirit of modern thought. To go into this profoundly exciting problem requires a preparatory groundwork which we cannot now provide. But let us say this much; that the nature of the living God is such that not only do our souls find in Him their eternal home, but our risen humanity also.

∞

Such an understanding of its meaning stamps the Christian life with a new character. It makes it concrete, alive, and concerned with men and things in a new way. It becomes true reality and acquires new warmth. The power that governs it is not the spirit, but the heart. By *heart,* we mean something radically different from emotionalism and sentimentality. The heart is that living union of blood and spirit that characterizes man. It is his center, the source of his becoming and, by conversion, re-becoming.

The central position of man in Christianity confers on the sacraments, especially on the Eucharist, a meaning wholly new. What did Christ mean when He said, "He that eateth my flesh and drinketh my blood hath everlasting life, and I will raise him up on the last day"?[55] Why did He not say, "He

[55]John 6:55.

that attaches his spirit to my spirit, who undertakes to do my will?" Because what matters is not "spirit," but the living, human-divine reality of Christ, which has its point of decision precisely in that which any spiritualizing tendency first relinquishes—namely, the body, or, in the precise language of St. John, "the flesh"; because in man, it is the living whole that matters, not only the soul. The point of decision is the physical act of eating and drinking, in contrast to any attempts at vaporizing this solid reality. The fruit of this sacred eating and drinking is the resurrection on the last day. Truly a "hard" saying, for it involves the end and purpose of the Christian life.

The doctrine of the Eucharist is guaranteed by the doctrine of the resurrection.

If with these assumptions and conclusions in mind, one wishes to summarize in one article the contents of the Christian Faith, one might securely say: "I believe in the resurrection of the body and the life everlasting," or, more precisely, "in its everlasting life." This is the last article in the Apostles' Creed, followed by the *Amen*, and rightly, for it is the sum and conclusion of all.

How God will judge us

God's will is fragile in the world

To clear our minds on the subject of the judgment, we should first have a better understanding of the nature of this earthly existence of ours, which we call history.

The historical order signifies above all a state of being that is both shut off and obscure. The whole web of causes and effects can neither be surveyed as a whole, nor can it be clearly grasped and understood. Into every action enter innumerable premises; the accomplished act in turn works its consequences in labyrinthine and hidden ways, few of which can be brought to light. Every occurrence is intertwined with many others and, finally, with all the rest. To understand an event rightly requires an overall view, but the outlines spread so far that no single view can encompass them. It is equally impossible to pierce through to the hidden depth. Beneath each level lies a deeper one, and since an event to be thoroughly known needs to be traced to its roots, it remains in large part uncomprehended.

Everything, again, that is alive can be known only by its outward expression. The life within finds ever-fresh expression without; the hidden life makes itself known by perceptible signs. But this is only one side of the question. Life is quite as liable to hide inside itself and to conceal its true nature. With plants and animals this play between expression and retraction is under nature's guidance and kept to a wise equilibrium. But with men the will enters in, and the will is perverse. Often what is within remains hidden when it should be manifested; the outward appearance does not correspond to the inward intention; purposes are veiled and become questionable. "Expression" may become the reverse of its purpose and lead to illusion. We can also hide ourselves from ourselves and live in self-delusion about our own purposes. The result is a state of obscurity, a sphere of ambiguity and error, impenetrable to the human eye, discouraging the application of rational judgment. History, in effect, is impenetrable, obscure, baffling to the understanding, tricky, and full of snares.

Yet history's purport is to make God known. What Paul says of nature, that "the invisible things of Him, from the creation of the world, are clearly seen, being understood by the things that are made," should also apply to the acts and destiny of mankind. The world of men, far more than the world of nature, should show forth "the everlasting power also and divinity of the Creator."[56] But the human will throws the whole into confusion, with the consequence that history at one and the same time seems aimless and meaningless, and again purposeful and leading to the truth of things. Consequently it may as easily turn the unenlightened heart away from God as guide it to Him.

[56]Cf. Rom. 1:20.

God's will is fragile in the world

∞

Our life in history proves that the human will is free. The will is free not only in small matters of preference but in issues of the gravest import. Above all, it is free to make the ultimate decision, the choice that effects the final purpose of man's life. Man is under a summons to do what is good, yet he must do it of his own free choice. And being free, he may leave the good undone, or may act contrary to it. Freedom makes it possible for a man to decide for God, or against Him. This freedom of ours, however, is by its very nature transitory and questionable. Yet it has to be if that true freedom is to be won in which the mind sees the good so clearly, and the heart is so abundantly filled with it, that there is no desire or will for anything else.

Freedom is the determining factor for the nature of history. It is the state of being in which a man ought to will the good, but has the capacity for willing the evil. To will evil most often means to will something that in itself is good, but not good at the time, or under the circumstances, or at the place or to the degree that good order requires. It is within the historical order that we may judge and act so mistakenly. And to the historical order belongs the even worse possibility of revolting against the good, of delighting in evil, and of willing and desiring destruction.

In the last analysis, the good is God's holiness itself. The obligation laid upon us that the good should be done is the same thing as God's will that the world should be His kingdom. As the sum of all man's actions, history ought to be the accomplishment of the good, the bringing about of the reign of holiness. If this were the case, man's nature would find in history its fulfillment. Out of man's actions the world would come to be what it was meant to be. But since man is free, his historical existence, his existence in time, is in jeopardy. We say that God's will cannot be frustrated. It may not be frustrated by nature, but it may be by free humanity. God intended His creatures to be truly free; He consented to expose His will to the possibility of frustration, and this possibility has not ceased to exist. But God's will is His own self. God does not stand above history in Olympian unconcern. He is involved in it, although in a way hard to define, and all the more deeply when He tells us that His will is love.

∞

History has another quality which at first we take as self-evident, but which, on close scrutiny, becomes most disconcerting. Might and right in no way conform to each other. Right is the reason for a thing to exist, the reason that justifies specific actions. Eating is justified as a means of maintaining life. Exertion on behalf of a friend has loyalty as its reason; strenuous application of thought, the search for truth. These right and worthy acts, wisely performed, are in keeping with the good. Goodness is the soul and essence of all values. Since the good is that highest worth which gives life its meaning, it would seem that it ought to impose itself immediately and without effort. This, however, is not the case. On the contrary, the assertion that "this is how things ought to be" generally evokes a smile. The higher the value in question, the greater its intrinsic worth and the less self-evident is its realization. Instinct easily sees to it that life is preserved, but some effort is required to maintain health and physical attractiveness. Loyalty, a more abstract virtue, demands sacrifice for its realization. And so, with every consecutive step on the ladder of values, the immediate might and power of the good diminishes.

∞

History is that state of being in which the higher the good, the less it imposes itself. Increasingly it must appeal to man's generosity, in order to see realized what is good and unselfish. It is of the essence of the fairy tale that goodness always has the power to realize itself. Children believe in this, and so does the child in each of us. To grow up, however, signifies that we acquire the bitter knowledge of experience. Then it will be seen that the good man is not always the strong man, the pure not always the healthy, as it should be. Neither is the noble and generous man always rich and honored, nor the fighter for the right, always victorious. Reality does not express the true purpose of things; success is not necessarily proof of merit; good fortune is not always the reward of virtue; beauty may be perilously independent of goodness. Whatever expression one may give to this oppressive mystery, the fact remains that as long as we live within the historical order, the intended order and the actual order do not coincide.

In the last analysis, what all this amounts to is that in history God Himself, in the immediately perceptible sense, is powerless, because He willed a free humanity, and respects its freedom. God's truth and holiness are ever present in history, yet man may ignore them; he may say that God "is not to his taste," that "God is dead." All this he may do, yet he will not be struck down by lightning, nor will he be swallowed up alive, nor will the world be thrown out of joint. God Himself has to appeal to man's generosity. One of the profoundest attractions of religion is that saintly chivalry that takes up arms for Him who is powerless in this world.

Three facts, then, mark the character of history: that it is obscure, that men are free to do wrong, and that evil may at times prevail over good. History cannot, therefore, be its own fulfillment. It points beyond itself. Man's most intimate desire, whether he acknowledges it or not, is that finally light should be thrown on so much obscurity and ambiguity, that the possibility of evil should be canceled out in true freedom, that the good may become the rule of reality, and that evil may at last be exposed for the nothingness and void that it is. In short, man must desire the judgment.

There is an ineradicable longing for justice which is part and parcel of our being—not in the petty sense alone that we will get what we pay for, or that our wrongs will be righted, but in a much deeper sense. We long that justice be done for its own sake, as regards ourselves personally, and as regards everyone else, and the world as a whole. Life must be brought under justice; the world should become what it ought to be. This we long for, although we know that the fulfillment of that wish may well turn against ourselves, since we are not only the victims of injustice, but also its instruments. When man calls out for justice, he calls out against himself; nevertheless he calls out. He has to desire that justice be done, even if it should cause his own perdition.

God alone can judge the world

At all periods of time men have been conscious that at the end of the historical process, there must be a judgment which concludes history and also fulfills it. Let us now inquire how the Christian gospel understands this Last Judgment.

Men and things will appear in their true light, as they are, and every deception will vanish. The inner and most hidden nature, both good and evil, will appear plainly, with all trappings stripped away. Every being will attain to what it is in truth.

No longer will it be possible to will evil. God will have made the good so manifest that men no longer will be able to shut it out. Their eyes and their minds will be so filled with it that they will not be able to help seeing that good alone has a right to exist. Evil will no longer appear as "necessary," or expedient, or as part of a full life, or as heroic, or as anything but what it really is—namely, unnecessary.

In the exact measure of its truth and goodness, each thing will be effective, alive, beautiful, and blessed. Truth and goodness, having become one with power, will triumphantly burst forth and everywhere prevail. Falsehood and evil will not only be punished, but will be forced out of effective operation by the omnipotence of holiness, without, however, being entirely obliterated. And this will be their damnation.

But how shall all this come about? By what process will the universe be judged?

∞

Of the various answers offered to the question, we will take up the three most prevalent ones.

The first answer is that history is its own judgment, since it tends to push events to their conclusion. Each action has consequences which again produce further consequences, and so a chain of cause and effect is set in motion which, little by little, brings the hidden into the open and separates the good from the bad. In the struggle between good and evil, the good motives must finally conquer because they are in accord with the laws of being. Since all being strives for the good, in the long run, a line of progress becomes discernible and at last there comes into clear view the end toward which the long process tended. And although the good may never be fully realized, and although all history is but an approach to the unattainable, still good exerts an effective force at all times and in all places.

This notion, although set forth with much confidence and persuasiveness, does not correspond to reality. History is not so constituted that in its process, motives are made indubitably plain. A true statement may work for the good in one hearer and may work mischief in another, according to their differing dispositions and attitudes. How can one assess its value? And may it not deteriorate further as one hearer passes a statement on to the next, and he to still others? Again, does a life necessarily become more intelligible as it grows longer? May not an old man be as blind and self-deceiving about his motives as a younger one—even blinder and more deceiving?

And as to results—are they not as concealing as they are revealing, sometimes beyond the power of critical assessment? For causes issue in results not only from thing to thing, but from person to person. Between things, the process is one of simple causality, and effects really disclose causes. But with persons, a force comes into play which is beyond the power of causality to reckon, namely, freedom.

Actually, the historical process begins anew with every human being. It is freedom that determines whether, in the long run, good or evil prevails. Sometimes evil will seem to be in such powerful possession that the honest good man finds himself looking like a fool. But even admitting that in the end, the historical process brings the whole to light, its claim to be a *judgment* would be in no way justified, for judgment requires justice. True judgment demands that every individual receive his just deserts, and likewise every period of time, every nation, and each for itself, singly, and not as part of a whole.

It is impossible to be sure toward what end history is moving, or, indeed, whether it is self-directed toward any goal at all. There are good reasons for saying that its meaning is becoming increasingly clear and good reasons for asserting the contrary, or that history takes its course without any perceivable meaning at all. Each assessment depends not on actual reasons, but on whether one is young and optimistic, or old and disillusioned, or sick or well or creative or unproductive. As a result, each point of view is often reversed to the statement that there is no reliable yardstick concerning value and worth, just as we have no reliable standard for measuring good and evil. Good is what gets results, valuable is what is effective; and if something is doomed to destruction, this in itself is proof that it no longer had any right to exist. By such standards, everything becomes relative, and life is deprived of all moral significance.

∞

Another assessment of history states that things happen according to necessity. The strong puts down the weak; the clever gets the better of the slow-witted, and the resourceful, of the simple-minded. Talk about good and evil is out of place where we are concerned with the historical process. Moral judgments belong to the inner life. Judgment consists in self-assessment as to one's intentions and spiritual worth. Such judgment, indeed, appears over the head of earthly events and their confusion, over the harsh obscurity of this world, beyond inescapable necessity, to a higher order where truth and spirit prevail and where the human heart comes into its own. This higher order is bound up with the idea of eternal life and hovers somewhere above man and beyond death.

This view of the historical process abandons the unity of existence. It divides life into two separate regions. One half is given over to natural necessity and to the ineluctable action of cause and effect. In the other half, worth and goodness are standards of measurement, and the heart receives its due. Between the two there is no connection. In order to enter the world of truth, one has to leave behind earthly existence and its confusion, "illusionary being." This is an acknowledgment of defeat. If we inquire more closely into the place of this order of truth and freedom, into the terms of admission valid for it, and into the methods by which it establishes justice, either there is no answer, or we encounter vague notions such as "spirit," "highest reality," and "eternal righteousness"—all of which are plainly recognizable as specters of Christian thought.

∞

The third answer is that given by the various religions. For them the judgment of the individual comes at his death, and the judgment of the world will come once the temporal order is finished. All shall then come into the presence of the Deity. The Deity is on the side of truth and goodness. Its eyes will pierce through the obscurity and confusion of things earthly, and each man's sentence will be pronounced, and his due will be apportioned to him.

What this notion is meant to convey is difficult to express. The development it has taken in the course of time, its entry into general philosophical and ethical ideas, demonstrates that it stands mainly for the belief that existence is subject to a moral order which will eventually and indisputably assert itself. In the end, truth will conquer, and each and every thing will be evaluated according to its true worth. Only, here again, the process breaks apart—into a *before* and *after* the death of the individual, a *before* and *after* the end of the world. This view, also, contains an element which can be satisfactorily solved only in the light of revealed religion: life, of itself, cannot reach clarification; a superior power must take hold of it and subject it to judgment. The clarification, the explanation, the final sentence, all of which are implied in *judgment*, are not the product of a vague spirituality, but of religion. The power that judges the world is not merely "truth" or "the morally good," but holiness. In the last analysis, the finality of judgment is not a product of correct insight into and evaluation of human life and history, but the outcome of the assumption of full authority over all being and existence by the divine power of holiness.

We will be judged by
our fidelity to Christ

Near the end of His life, during His last visit to Jerusalem, Jesus spoke these words: "And immediately after the tribulation of those days, the sun shall be darkened and the moon shall not give her light, and the stars shall fall from heaven, and the powers of Heaven shall be moved. And then shall appear the sign of the Son of Man in Heaven; and then shall all tribes of the earth mourn; and they shall see the Son of Man coming in the clouds of Heaven with much power and majesty. And He shall send His angels with a trumpet, and a great voice: and they shall gather together His elect from the four winds, and from the farthest parts of the heavens to the utmost bounds of them."[57]

And again: "When the Son of Man shall come in His majesty, and all the angels with Him, then shall He sit upon the seat of His majesty. And all nations shall be gathered together before Him, and He shall separate them one from another, as

[57]Matt. 24:29-31.

the shepherd separateth the sheep from the goats. And He
shall set the sheep on His right hand, but the goats on His
left. Then shall the King say to them that shall be on His
right hand: 'Come, ye blessed of my Father, possess the kingdom prepared for you from the foundation of the world. For I
was hungry, and you gave me to eat; I was thirsty, and you gave
me to drink; I was a stranger, and you took me in; naked, and
you covered me; sick, and you visited me; I was in prison, and
you came to me.' Then shall the just answer Him, saying:
'Lord, when did we see Thee hungry, and feed Thee; thirsty,
and gave Thee drink? And when did we see Thee a stranger,
and take Thee in? Or naked, and cover Thee? Or when did we
see Thee sick, or in prison, and come to Thee?' And the King
answering, shall say to them: 'Amen I say to you, as long as
you did it to one of these, my least brethren, you did it to me.'

And then He shall say to them also that shall be on His
left hand: 'Depart from me, you cursed, into the everlasting
fire which was prepared for the Devil and his angels. For I
was hungry, and you gave me not to eat; I was thirsty, and you
gave me not to drink. I was a stranger, and you took me not
in; naked, and you covered me not; sick and in prison, and
you did not visit me.' Then they also shall answer Him, saying:
'Lord, when did we see Thee hungry, or thirsty, or a stranger,
or naked, or sick, or in prison, and did not minister to Thee?'
Then He shall answer them, saying: 'Amen, I say to you, as
long as you did it not to one of these least, neither did you do
it unto me.' And these shall go into everlasting punishment,
but the just into life everlasting."[58]

[58]Matt. 25:31-46.

If we shake off the seeming familiarity which comes from having heard them often, these passages strike us suddenly as strange and disconcerting. This is not how we should expect things to be. Here premises are taken for granted to which we are not sure we can give assent. But if we have some acquaintance with Revelation, and know enough of men to treat certain of their unconscious assumptions with caution— and these are the first steps in Christian knowledge—it is this very feeling that here is something disconcerting that alerts us to the fact that we are face to face with an essential and crucial element in our Faith. The disconcerting element here lies in the concrete, the personal approach.

The habit of the modern mind is to take seriously only that kind of thinking that interprets everything in terms of natural necessity or of intellectual laws. Existence for us has become a system of matter and energy, of law and natural order. Every process takes place within that system. Children or simple folk may think of natural objects as being manipulated by superior beings, as they are in legends and fairy tales, but the educated adult does not. For him the first condition of intelligent thinking is to conceive of the universe as an interconnection of physical and spiritual laws, which govern man and his destinies as well as the historical process.

If a final judgment is posited—a procedure, that is, by which the life and deeds of man are scrutinized, judged, and given their eternal value—we would have to think of it as a judgment in which man, or more properly his spirit, comes into the unveiled light of God, and in that light, his life becomes transparent, and his worth is made evident.

Eternal Life

In Jesus' discourse on the Last Judgment, however, this is not at all what takes place. The judge is not an abstract deity, an all-wise, all-righteous spirit, but Christ, the Son made man. Nor does man, by the mere fact of his death, or the world, simply by coming to an end, appear before God. Rather, it is Christ who "cometh." He comes to the world and wrests it from a condition in which "this-sidedness" and the subjection to natural law make possible the obscurity of history. A final investigation is carried out which brings all existing things into the presence of Christ. Men, not only their spirits, appear before Him—men in their concrete, soul-and-body actuality; and not individual men only, but "the world." In order to make this possible, the body—the deceased, corrupt body—rises up from the dead, not by any natural necessity, but in obedience to the summons of Christ. And the act of judgment is not simply illumination in the eternal light and holiness of God, but an act of Jesus Christ, who was once upon earth and now reigns in eternal glory. He reviews mankind in its whole history, as well as each particular man, passes judgment, and assigns to each man that form of being which accords with his worth in the sight of God.

∞

To modern man, all this appears as sheer fantasy—at best as symbol. To his mentality, this kind of thinking is on the level of children and primitives. Mythology, folklore, and fairy tales treat universal processes in this anthropomorphic manner, that is, as modeled on human conduct. Children, as soon as they grow up, and primitive people, when they become civilized, perceive that the universe is governed by inflexible laws and must be conceived of in philosophical or scientific terms. The Christian teaching of the Last Judgment is just a myth and must give way to a more serious and advanced view of reality.

Again we have to decide where we stand with regard to Revelation. Are we to confine our Faith to our emotions, and adapt our thinking to that of current views, or shall we be Christians in our minds also? For what modern man describes as childish, primitive, and anthropomorphic is the essential, distinguishing quality of our Faith. For when the worth of the world and of history are finally determined, it will not be by universal natural or spiritual laws, nor by confrontation with an absolute, divine reality, but by a divine *act*. Let it be well understood—by an *act*, and not through the workings of some force of nature or spirit, just as the economy of salvation does not rest upon some higher natural order but upon a direct intervention of God, which takes place in the sphere of human history and finds constant expression in this sphere; and just as the world did not evolve as a natural reality from natural causes, but as God's work, summoned into being by His free and all-powerful word.

If we want to be Christians in our thinking also, then we cannot conceive of the relation of God to the world, to man, and to the whole of existence in terms derived from natural science or metaphysics, but only in concepts belonging to the personal sphere; that is, precisely in the despised anthropomorphic concepts of action, decision, destiny, and freedom. Such is the language of Scripture, and when a man has striven for truth with sufficient sincerity and above all with sufficient patience for false notions to fall away and things to show themselves in their true light, he comes to see that in the final sifting of values, what really meets the case are those so-called anthropomorphic concepts.

The judgment is the last in the series of God's acts. It proceeds from His free counsels, and is carried out by Him whose intervention in history was rejected by men at His appearance upon earth, but whose destiny, since God is faithful, accomplished our redemption. Throughout history, He has remained as a "sign that will be contradicted,"[59] as the touchstone for men and for nations. It is He who executes the judgment. He is doing it because He is God's Son, because He is the Word "through whom all things were made,"[60] and to whom the world belongs, whether the world acknowledges it or not.

∞

The strangeness which reverses our scientific and philosophic notions reaches still deeper. How does this judgment take place? On what is it based, and according to what standards does it determine a man's worth?

At first glance we might assume that what is judged would be a man's actions and omissions, his deeds as well as his character, the details as much as the whole, each according to the multiplicity of rules and norms pertaining to it. Instead, we see everything fused into only one thing: love — the love

[59]Luke 2:34.
[60]Cf. John 1:3.

that is aroused by compassion for man's need. And what is here in question is plainly that first and greatest commandment, and the second which is like unto it, as Jesus taught in the Gospel, the commandment of love, of which the apostle speaks as of "the fulfilling of the law."[61] Consequently, although it is only the love for one's neighbor that is mentioned, the commandment includes the whole realm of love; only love is spoken of, but this love includes doing and becoming and being what is right.

How will this standard of love be established and applied? The judge, we might suppose, would say, "You have obeyed the law of love and are therefore accepted," or, "You have denied the law of love, and are therefore rejected." What He says, however, is, "You are accepted because you have shown love to me; you are rejected because you denied me love." This, too, is comprehensible, we might answer, since love is the first commandment and should be practiced toward all men, and since Christ, who enjoins this commandment and fulfilled it Himself to the uttermost, has placed Himself, as it were, behind each man to lend final weight to each individual being.

This might well be so, but once we examine the context without bias, we find that this is not what Christ teaches. The highest standard of love is not the love Christ preaches and to which all are obligated, including Christ Himself; the highest standard of love is Christ Himself. It begins in Him and persists through Him. Outside of Christ, it is nonexistent, and philosophical disquisitions on the subject have as

[61]Matt. 22:37-39; Rom. 13:10.

little to do with this kind of love as He who in the New Testament is called the Father has to do with "the divinity of the heavenly sphere" or the concept of "cause and effect" has to do with God's Providence.

∞

Now there opens before us the uniqueness, the awesomeness and, yes, the scandal of the Christian meaning of *judgment:* man will be judged according to his relationship to Christ. Truthfulness, justice, faithfulness, chastity, and whatever else is considered ethical are in their deepest meaning the right relationship to Christ. If we speak of truth, we imply a general attitude of the mind, namely, the fact that we recognize something in the light of eternal reality. But in the prologue to his Gospel, John gives us to understand that this interpretation of truth is but an interpolated, conditional link. Ultimately, truth is the Word, the *Logos* Himself, and knowledge, accordingly, is knowing the *Logos*, Christ, and all things in Him.

The same applies to judgment. If we speak of goodness, we imply the highest value; and by *right conduct*, we understand the realization of good. But according to the discourse on the Last Judgment, Christ is the good, and to do good means to love Christ. Truth and goodness, in the final analysis, are no mere abstract values and concepts, but someone—Jesus Christ. Reversing the approach, we might say that every intimation of truth, however fragmentary, is also the beginning of a knowledge of Christ. Similarly, any charitable action is directed toward Christ, and reaches Him in the end, just as any wicked action, whatever its immediate context, is, in the end, an attack upon Him. Goodness may shine out in various places, in man, things, and events; but in its essence it shines forth Jesus Christ. The doer need have no thought of Christ; he may think of other people only, but his act ultimately reaches Christ. He need not even know Christ and may never have heard of Him, yet what is done is done to Christ.

To pierce with His glance the width of the whole world and the course of thousands of years, the life of each man and of each nation and community, to judge and affix to each the meaning it bears eternally, is God's act of doom. Christ will come and execute that judgment. It will be irrevocable because it is true, because it is the exact account without remainder of every man, every community of men. It is irrevocable also because it is an act of power as much as of truth, power that is absolute and irresistible. By this judgment the state of man and of mankind will be settled before God forever.

But Christ is not only Judge; He is also Redeemer. Even as Judge He is Redeemer. The judgment is not the revenge of the offended Son of God, not His personal triumph over His enemies. By saying that truth and goodness are a person— Christ—it is not suggested that any personal element would intrude and blur the impartial validity of truth and goodness. The judgment is justice, yet not justice in and for itself, but justice bound up with the living mind and love of Christ. The Last Judgment is the fulfillment of redemption.

∞

The vastness of such a view of things is overwhelming. It disrupts and reverses modern thinking and its conception of existence as the expression of natural law or a philosophical system. It is not ideas and laws that matter, but reality. The most real of realities is a person, the Son of God made man. He is what He was, Jesus of Nazareth. But He will be manifest as Lord, mightier than the world, greater than history, and more comprehensive than all that is called idea, value, or moral law. These things exist and are valid, but only as rays from His light.

The doctrine of the Last Judgment is, at bottom, a revelation of Christ. It shows us, too, the task which confronts us if we want to be Christians in the true sense of the word. It implies seeing Christ in everything, carrying His image in our hearts with such intensity that it lifts us above the world, above history and the works of men, and enables us to see those things for what they are, to weigh them and assign to them their eternal value — in a word, to be their judges.

What it means to
dwell in eternity

In time we can find foretastes of eternity

Eternity is a term all but debased by modern usage. It is applied all too freely, often as a mere catchword for the mysterious and important. Depreciation of this kind is an evil. A word is not merely a sign to convey a meaning. It is a living thing, embodying spirit. In company with other words, it makes up language, and language is the room in which man lives. It is the world of mental images from which the light of truth is ever breaking upon him. When a word decays, it is not merely that we become uncertain of each other's meaning. One of the forms that compose our life has perished. A signpost has become illegible. A light has been extinguished and our intellectual day made darker. To restore to its original meaning a word that is being destroyed by careless use is a service to the whole of human life. With this premise in mind let us now ask: What is the real meaning of *eternity*?

Our first reaction to this question is that it means unending time. We speak of the eternal stars, of man's eternal suffering, of the eternal recurrence of things. This is much the

sense in which the term is used in the mythological represen-
tations of the afterlife. In the belief of hunting and herding
peoples, the dead go to the happy hunting ground and pursue
there the same life they lived on earth, only in a higher and
more wonderful fashion, and lasting forever. Other peoples,
by placing in their graves the things the dead had valued in
life (jewels, furniture, boats, slaves—the real objects or rep-
resentations of them), showed that they thought of eternity
as a never-ending continuation of earthly existence.

Ostensibly, *eternity* signifies time prolonged forever. This
is a misconception we can hardly dispense with in ordinary
thinking. We know that time is limited, that it is measured
by hours, days, and years, and however we increase or decrease
the unit of measurement, it still remains limited. Yet we can
no more represent to ourselves an end of earthly time than we
can a beginning. The beginning and the end—both are mys-
teries with which, of ourselves, we are not equipped to deal.
To our sense, time goes on and on, backward as well as for-
ward. Religious mythology makes a mystery of this continuation, and religious sentiment veils the inconsistency.

∞

Yet the authentic meaning of *eternity* is the abolition of
time. That is easily said, but impossible to imagine. It can be
grasped only intellectually, in the way a mathematical statement is grasped. Is timelessness compatible with existence?
What would be left of life with time removed? Could a state
of things be real which neither comes into being nor ceases
to be, which knows no change and yet is without fixity, is

alive and fruitful? Perhaps it might; "timeless moments" have been experiences which give at least an intimation of what such a state might be.

∞

There is such a thing as mechanical time. It is a mere succession of moments, regardless of their content—comparable to a riverbed run dry. It is represented by the clock with its indifference to what passes, with its cold insensibility, which, although so alien to the joys and sorrows of the human heart, yet for that very reason impresses us so powerfully.

But this is not time as we humans experience it; that time, as we live it, is alive also. It is really the only time we know, and the threat we sense in the irrevocable, impassible movements of the hands of the clock derives from the fact that it is our lifetime that it is measuring out. Mechanical time stands, as it were, as a margin around our lifestream, as an external means of measurement. But in the immediate experience of our own temporal passage, time is an entirely different thing. An hour filled with rich experience and an hour spent in boredom and emptiness are not perceived as time segments of equal length. One passes in an instant; the other drags on endlessly. In retrospect the impression is reversed. The hour that passed so tediously shrinks to nothingness; the hour that sped by with the momentum of strong emotion expands in the memory.

Consequently, when one's own life is concerned, time takes on a new character. It is a succession of events, but it is not, as with the mechanically propelled hands of the clock, a meaningless sequence. Time-experience varies in meaning, depth, and intensity, as it bears upon our own unique existence—an existence linked to the dignity and responsibility of the person. It is measured not only by the hands of the clock but also by what is contained within it.

What, we ask now, are the potentialities of this kind of experienced time?

A fairy tale tells of a magician who asked a caliph to dip his face into a basin of water. The caliph did as he was told, and lived a full life's experience, followed by a succession of other lives—as a man, a woman, a water-carrier, a sage, and so on. During the last existence something startled him, and he noticed that he was just lifting his face from the basin. In the brief space of time measured by the necessity of drawing breath, he had lived an immeasurable amount of life.

This may be a fairy tale, but it is a meaningful one. If we consider the relation between the two kinds of time—one of content, one of duration; one measured by importance, one by happenings only—might it not be possible to suppose that by compressing the spread of one to a flash and increasing the significance of the other to the highest intensity, the line of movement would thus not come to an end, but would point to what it is in reality—eternity? Eternity, then, would be a state of life in which nothing just passes by, but all is simultaneously present, in which there is no succession of moments and events, but simultaneous happening only, yet which on account of the momentousness of the content and the intensity and perfection of experience precludes all tedium.

In time we can find foretastes of eternity

∞

Let us now consider another experience. Life contains, as one of its elements, an urge to speed, either to fly from danger or to pursue some coveted goal. But it also contains the impulse of release from action, from inner and outer compulsion. There are moments—all too few—of perfect inner serenity, when desire and fear are suspended, and it seems difficult to understand why one has striven so hard or been so afraid. A step further, one feels, and the restless current will be stilled in the timeless moment, stilled because it has had its fill, not of this or that, not of things that delude or disappoint, but of life and being itself, simple and all-embracing. This, too, is an attempt of life to transcend time and find the absolute present. It never succeeds. These timeless moments are always interrupted either from without or from within. But they give us a hint in the direction toward eternity.

∞

Take still a third experience. I have a practical task, I accomplish it satisfactorily, and all is settled. My only reaction is the knowledge that a specific goal has been reached and that I can now go ahead to the next step without further worry. But when it is a matter of moral obligation, my reaction is quite different. Here I know that I am dealing with an absolute, I give my assent to it, and I do what must be done. An action that is purely practical is ended when its goal is reached; the more utilitarian the purpose, the more final the accomplishment. But in the case of moral obligation, we are conscious that we touch the absolute. Utility vanishes, once the object is reached; goodness is permanent, of a permanence that is not measured in days and years, or in terms of memory. It is timeless. And the more a man wills the absolute, the more he himself participates in its character. The more firmly and energetically he strives for the good, the more he grows into the nature of this absolute—goodness. Consequently, if a man willed a thing wholly good in itself, and willed it in complete candor with all his heart, pouring into this willing and this doing the full measure of his vital strengths, a mysterious thing would happen. He would have passed into eternity.

∞

From experiences such as these grows a notion of what eternity might be: the perfect still point of perfect being. There would be neither development nor decline. Everything that lives would realize its full potentialities in the simple act of being. Appearance and capacities would be equally and fully valid. At every point, existence would be justified by its worth. Not only would it *be,* but it would be rightfully.

Of himself man cannot attain to this state of eternity. His own capacities are insufficient to reach a wholly living present in which goodness is perfectly realized. If there existed a being whose whole purpose was absolute goodness, a being as powerful as it was good, a being perfectly good, perfectly great, there would be no change nor striving in such an existence. The life would be filled with meaning, and its purpose with reality. There would be no movement from or toward— the present alone would become absolute. There is such a being—it is God—and the mode of His being is eternity. Time is not an element that surrounds us, a channel through which we travel. We ourselves—our finiteness—are time. Eternity is God's mode of living.

Therefore, eternity is not ours by nature, although we are directed toward it and long for it. Our participation in it depends on our relationship to God. But in what manner?

Father, Son, and Holy Spirit dwell in eternity

It is the teaching of pantheistic mysticism—Indian, Persian, and neo-Platonic—that man, by means of purification, contemplation, cognition, and self-denial, may reach a point where he becomes one with the deity, where he takes on the form of Godhead. At this point he is withdrawn from time, and becomes eternal like God. But such is not the language of Christian Revelation.

In this point, too, Christianity takes that characteristic turn from the universal and metaphysical to the personal and historical that gives the contemporary mind a sensation of retrogression, as if things divine were adjusted to human measure, were made popular or childish, or primitive. Noble and profound though it may sound to think of the final reality as the life substance existing in the still present of the Absolute Mind, and to think of the righteous human spirit as abandoning the transient and individual in order to become absorbed into that ineffable life, such a view deprives man of the fundamental truth of his existence according to which

God alone is God, and man is unequivocally a creature. In the parables and figures of the gospel, which present that basic truth, the eternal life of the creature is represented as a hymn of praise; as a service before God, and a reigning with God;[62] as an entering of God into man's life—God taking up His abode with him;[63] as a wedding feast to which the whole world is invited.[64] What is meant by these comparisons?

The answer might be that those parables express the very mystical and metaphysical conception of eternity spoken of before. Actually this is the opinion of some religious thinkers famed for the profoundness of their insight. In reality, however, they miss and destroy the genuine meaning. Of course such figures of speech are symbolic, for in eternity no hymns will be sung, no banquet table spread where men sit as guests; not symbolic but precise and literal, however, is the statement that eternity is not a metaphysical reference that may be expressed through such concepts as "truth," "essence," and "life," but that it is a relation between persons. In this lies the special message of the gospel. Let us try once more to find, among our everyday experiences, parallels which would serve to clarify the meaning.

∞

In a room there is a table with chairs, a cupboard against the wall, and a lamp hanging from the ceiling. This is a physical

[62]Rev. 3:5 and 22:3-5.
[63]John 14:23.
[64]Cf. Rev. 19:7-9.

room, which contains various objects—close together, coordinated, above and below.

Now another instance: I am sitting on a bench outdoors. Everything is quiet, I am peaceful and relaxed. My thoughts take a pleasant turn, and I experience the sensation of space. This space is not only all around me, in the countryside, but also inside me. Here again is a room, but of another kind, in which there are also things—the inner life, with its fluctuations, emotions, and the like.

Another instance: I am turning a problem over in my mind, examining it with care in all its aspects, comparing, distinguishing, and combining. Suddenly the truth dawns with its very own power of persuasiveness—truth in itself, self-sufficing, independent from end, object, or purpose. Here again is a room of a new kind, which also contains something—the room of the intellect, furnished with my thoughts or, more properly, my knowledge, or more precisely still, myself as a being that lives by truth.

Now, as a last instance, take two people who have known and liked each other for years, have worked together and shared all kinds of experiences. Suddenly one of them makes an unexpected observation. The other, startled, thinks: "So that's what you are really like." He suddenly has the other "in focus." This is not a perception of the exterior, which he has always seen, for he is not blind. Neither is it a perception commanding recognition and esteem—all this has been granted long ago. Rather, it is that lightning stroke of insight with which a person suddenly "sees" the underlying reality of another person. Again a new room is opened in which two people are together in a new way—the room of mutual personal understanding, of respect, loyalty, love, and friendship. Man may live in all four rooms. As body, he lives in the physical room; as a being with perception and feeling, in the room of life; as an intellectual nature, in the room of truth and beauty; and, since he can gain insight into another person, in the room of personal relationships.

In Holy Scripture we find such things as the following: "In the beginning was the Word, and the Word was with God, and the Word was God. The same was in the beginning with God."[65] It does not say the Word was with God "formerly" or "once"; it does not make use of any time-measuring term. It plainly says, "In the beginning." This beginning is not the first of a series of moments in time; it is the beginning, simply, of God's original kingdom. It is the mode of God's existence—eternity. What determines it? What is the "room" of God's existence? Not the physical room, or the room of animal life (of perception and feeling)—obviously not. And not the intellectual room either. Not even John, who is given to saying that God is "the truth,"[66] "love,"[67] and "the light,"[68] has said, "In the beginning, God was in His absolute truth."

He describes God's existence in these words, "The Word was with God." By *God* is meant the Father; by *Word*, the Son. He, the Son, is "with" the Father. And lest the language should dissolve in metaphysics, at the end of the prologue John says, "No man hath seen the Father at any time; the

[65]John 1:1-2.
[66]John 14:6.
[67]1 John 4:8.
[68]1 John 1:5.

only-begotten Son, who is in the bosom of the Father, He hath declared Him."[69] The two, humanly speaking, are *with* one another and are turned toward each other in mutual understanding of infinite knowledge and love. The knowledge is not apprehension, but comprehension; the love is a love which each owes wholly to the other, and yet it is perfectly free.

This independence, this unity, this loyalty, and this intimacy are made possible by the Holy Spirit. Only through the Holy Spirit is the Son truly Himself, and the Father also Himself, for it is the Holy Spirit who effects the omnipotent fruitfulness and freedom of the divine birth. Only in the Holy Spirit are Father and Son one God. For it is the work of the Holy Spirit that the Son was begotten—that He does not turn from, but toward the Father—and that He is with the Father and abides with Him. This relation that is between the Father and the Son, this room in which Father and Son so turn toward one another, and so abide in one another—this is the final, the real, eternity.

Such a room is revealed in the Gospel where we are told that when Jesus was baptized, "He came up out of the water; and lo, the heavens were opened to Him: and He saw the Spirit of God descending as a dove and coming upon Him. And behold, a voice from Heaven saying: 'This is my beloved Son in whom I am well pleased.' "[70] "The heavens were opened," the room, the place set aside for the unapproachable

[69]John 1:18.
[70]Matt. 3:16-17.

light,[71] where God is alone with Himself; that place is opened. From there the Father looks down upon the Son and speaks words of knowledge and love. There, too, the Son turns to the Father, comprehends His will and takes the responsibility for His veneration upon Himself. Here, again, is the eternal, divine interrelatedness, the "I" and the "Thou." The room that spreads between and around Them—its intimacy, its stillness, is, properly, eternity.

Eternity is the center of all things. From it, all things proceed; to it, all things return.

[71]1 Tim. 6:16.

Christ unites us with
His Father in eternity

Whatever Paul and John have to say about the Christian life is built upon the relationship "man-in-Christ" and "Christ-in-man."

Primarily this means that the believer is enlightened and governed by the Spirit of the Lord. But it means more. By His death and Resurrection Christ passed into a new state. He became, in Paul's words, a spirit.[72] As a spirit, He is able, without destroying the solid substance of man's humanity, or canceling His individual interior life, or jeopardizing his dignity as a person, to be "in" the believer. He is in him as the image that forms him, as the power that governs him, as his support, and as the center from which he lives. In every Christian, in conformity with his state and his personality, the life of Christ is lived anew. It is Christ who lives in him, and for that very reason, it is the man, now for the first time in full possession of his personal humanity, that lives too.

[72]1 Cor. 15:45.

And again it is the Holy Spirit who creates the relationship. He created it first on the day of Pentecost, when He changed the weak and troubled disciples into Christians and Apostles, and from that day on, He creates it by faith and Baptism.

By faith and Baptism Christ's quickening being becomes the believer's own. Of this inexhaustible truth, the part that now concerns us is that the believer, by entering into communion with Christ, is admitted through Christ into His relationship with the Father. Christ has said, "No one knoweth the Son but the Father, neither doth anyone know the Father but the Son, and he to whom it shall please the Son to reveal Him";[73] and again, "No one can come to me unless the Father, who hath sent me, draw him";[74] and yet again, "I am the way, and the truth, and the life. No man cometh to the Father, but by me."[75]

The goal of all human progress is the Father. There is no other, and that goal includes all others. But the way to the Father does not lie open to our view. He is the highest creative power, the wisdom that governs all things—as natural religion divined—but His nature as Father is hidden. He is the unknown God. We know of Him only as much as He has revealed of Himself, and that much He has revealed in Christ. Through Christ we learn about the Father in that He is revealed in the Son. In his first letter, John says explicitly, "Whosoever denieth the Son, the same hath not the Father. He that confesseth the Son, hath the Father also."[76]

[73]Matt. 11:27.
[74]John 6:44.
[75]John 14:6.
[76]1 John 2:23.

∞

To be a child of God—let us say the words in full awareness of their grave import—to be God's son or daughter, means not only trusting God and loving Him and feeling oneself under His protection. It means a thing as plain as it is astounding. It means to be received through grace into that relation with the Father which is the Incarnate Son's by nature.

Paul presents the idea in all its force. To believe means to be seized by Christ, and not only psychologically, as a student may be influenced by a teacher, but in actuality. It is to be drawn by Him into His own life and into the living relationship to the Father in which He stands as Son. Thereby is the believer received into the reciprocal relationship between Father and Son. This may well be the ultimate meaning of Christ's saying, "I am the way." Christ does not say, "I will point out the way," or, "I go this way before you," but "I *am* the way." There is no way to the Father that exists in the natural order, or in human nature, apart from Christ. The way is not a connection between things, but a relation between persons. In the end it is the way of the Incarnation whereby one stands among us, Jesus Christ, who, being man as we are, is able to share our lives fully with us, and being God as none besides, is able to carry us over into a place reserved by God for Himself.

On earth these things are only in their beginnings, and still in the stage of effort and struggle. The new life in Christ is a hidden life, and we must believe in it and maintain it loyally, however it may be disclaimed by the appearances around us.

But a beginning has in truth been made, and the way leads over into that eternal life we speak of, in which Father and Son live one for the other in independence and union, in honor and love, in mutual knowledge and entire devotion. That deep and wide and holy communion is the home we are promised, where we rightfully belong. It is eternal life.

∞

The Last Judgment, with the events that precede it, brings history to its conclusion. The enclosure of time is broken open. The man of good will is received into the eternal life which, in the love of the Holy Spirit, is between Father and Son. This is the entering in by the door, the tarrying, the abiding, the marriage feast, the song of praise, the sacred service. This is that secret promise at the end of each of the seven letters in the book of Revelation made to those who are faithful and have overcome.[77] And that the same words that are used of "the only-begotten Son lying in the bosom of the Father"[78] are used again of the intimate affection between Jesus and the disciple whom He loved (where it is said that he leaned "on the breast of Jesus,"[79]) is, as it were, a foretaste and a pledge.

It was said in the chapter on the resurrection that it was not a soul or a spirit that was received into eternal life, but the whole human being with his soul-and-body nature, with

[77]Rev. 2:7.
[78]John 1:18.
[79]John 13:25.

his history, his particular destiny, his words and his acts, insofar as these were ratified by the judgment. Extraordinary as is
such a claim, it is but the last link of a chain that runs
through the gospel.

On the face of it, it seems incredible that a finite being
should be received into communion with God. It is a shock-
ing idea to anyone who has escaped from pantheism, with its
confusion of natures, and has come to see that all intellectual
precision depends on the recognition that God is God, and
man merely a creature, and that between them there is the
gulf of the difference of natures. In order that the eternal life
promised us may be possible, a wholly new element must enter in. This element is grace, in its full and absolute sense.

It seems equally incredible, at least to our modern sensi-
bilities, that this finite being should be the whole human being. It might be more thinkable if it were his spirit only—
although, in that case, we would be deceiving ourselves, for
the word *spirit* must not be used of God and man in the same
sense. If the human being is a spirit, God is one so different
and so incomprehensible that the gulf of incompatibility lies
between. In spite of this incompatibility, it seems more acceptable to think of the human spirit. Here, however, it has
been said that man's body, also, his human fate, his acts, his
works, performed in time and space—all this is to be received into the intimate life of the Godhead.

It sounds like a fairy tale. If it is, then the Resurrection
and the Ascension are also fairy tales. For He who dwells for
all eternity in the Father is not only the Logos; He is the
God-man, Jesus Christ, in all the plenitude of His redeeming
life. Although men have found it a scandal intolerable to

think of that the human frame of Christ should be taken up into the pure spirituality of God, the Church has waged war on behalf of that scandal with a keen awareness and an expenditure of energy that shows that the issue is final. For the whole Christian religion turns on these facts: that after the Resurrection Christ remained man; that as man He entered into eternal life; and that He lives in closest union with God, not as *Logos* only, but also as the glorified Jesus of Nazareth. God has created man and willed man to be in such a fashion that this is possible. Moreover, God is such that He could will it and make it possible. He is not the God of philosophers or pious spiritualists, but another altogether, a God not known to man and, for the first time, revealed to him in Christ. Equally unknown was the mystery of man, and that also was first made known by Christ.

In the eighth chapter of Romans and in the first part of the letters to the Ephesians and Colossians, we are told that not only is man to be drawn into the holy relationship we speak of, but the whole creation; that not man's redemption alone is in question, but also the world's; that not only is there to be a "new man," but also a "new Heaven and a new earth." This will come about not directly, as in magic or myth, but through the medium of man.

How extensive and intricate is the union between man and things I will not stop now to point out, except to say that it had its beginning in the doctrine of Providence. This doctrine does not say that the providential order is a higher stage of the natural order, but that when a man in faith brings his will into accord with the will of the Father, things about him are ordered anew in his regard. Every time this is done, a new beginning is made, and a new creature comes into being. As Paul writes in the eighth chapter of Romans: "For the expectation of the creature waiteth for the revelation of the sons of God. For the creature was made subject to vanity, not willingly, but by reason of Him that made it subject, in hope; because the creature also itself shall be delivered from the servitude of corruption, into the liberty of the glory of the children of God. For we know that every creature groaneth and travaileth in pain, even till now."[80]

On every side, created nature presses toward this beginning of light, which is that same relationship to the Father into which Christ brings man. In Ephesians, Paul speaks of "the mystery of His will, according to his good pleasure, which He hath purposed in Him, in the dispensation of the fullness of times, to re-establish all things in Christ, that are in Heaven and on earth."[81] The whole world, and not man only, is seized upon by the formative power of Christ. Thus the letter to the Colossians speaks of the "kingdom of the Son of His love, in whom we have redemption through His blood, the remission of sins; who is the image of the invisible God, the firstborn of every creature; for in Him were all things created in Heaven and on earth, visible and invisible, whether thrones, or dominations, or principalities, or powers; all things were created by Him and in Him. And He is before all, and by Him all things consist. And He is the head of the Body, the Church, who is the beginning, the firstborn from the dead; that in all things He may hold the primacy; because in

---

[80]Rom. 8:19-22.
[81]Eph. 1:9-10.

Him, it hath well pleased the Father, that all fullness [of creation] should dwell."[82] The whole of creation is here spoken of as moving on toward that hidden eternal life in question—somewhat as in the Platonic opinion of all nature striving back toward its original state through the Pan-Eros; but not without an intermediary: in the Christian doctrine, however, it is through man, through man's redeemed and converted heart.

In trying to set forth the Christian doctrine of eternal life we have used many words and many notions, and we still leave it far from clear, far from complete. And yet the matter is very simple.

One hears it said over and over that Christianity belittles man and holds the body in contempt, that it denies the value of the world and withdraws the believer from active work into spiritual and religious bypaths. It is difficult to understand how so false and unfounded an opinion got and maintained its hold. Nowhere is man looked upon as so great a being as in the Christian gospel; nowhere else is the world of such serious importance; nowhere else is the temporal order of creation so elevated toward God and in God as by and through Christ. The way this was done is untouched by any breath of myth or fable, and the guarantee of its seriousness, its divine seriousness, is the life and death of Christ.

[82]Col. 1:15-19.

Biographical note

Romano Guardini (1885-1968)

Although he was born in Verona, Italy, Romano Guardini
grew up in Mainz, Germany, where his father was serving as
Italian consul. Since his education and formation were German, he decided to remain in Germany as an adult.

After studying chemistry and economics as a youth,
Guardini turned to theology and was ordained to the priesthood
in 1910. From 1923 to 1939 (when he was expelled by the
Nazis), Father Guardini occupied a chair especially created
for him at the University of Berlin as "professor for philosophy of religion and Catholic *Weltanschauung*." After the war,
similar positions were created for him—first at the University
of Tübingen and then at the University of Munich (1948-63).

Father Guardini's extremely popular courses in these uni-
versities won him a reputation as one of the most remarkable
and successful Catholic educators in Germany. As a teacher,
a writer, and a speaker, he was notable for being able to de-
tect and nurture those elements of spirituality that nourish
all that is best in the life of Catholics.

Eternal Life

After the war, Father Guardini's influence grew to be enormous, not only through his university positions, but also through the inspiration and guidance he gave to the postwar German Catholic Youth Movement, which enlivened the faith of countless young people.

Father Guardini's writings include works on meditation, education, literature, art, philosophy, and theology. Among his dozens of books, perhaps the most famous is *The Lord*, which has been continuously in print in many languages since its first publication in 1937. Even today, countless readers continue to be transformed by these books, which combine a profound thirst for God with great depth of thought and a delightful perfection of expression. The works of Father Guardini are indispensable reading for anyone who wants to remain true to the Faith and to grow holy in our age of skepticism and corrosive doubt.

Sophia Institute Press®

Sophia Institute Press®

Sophia Institute is a nonprofit institution that seeks to restore man's knowledge of eternal truth, including man's knowledge of his own nature, his relation to other persons, and his relation to God.

Sophia Institute Press® serves this end in numerous ways. It publishes translations of foreign works to make them accessible for the first time to English-speaking readers. It brings back into print books that have been long out of print. And it publishes important new books that fulfill the ideals of Sophia Institute. These books afford readers a rich source of the enduring wisdom of mankind.

Sophia Institute Press® makes these high-quality books available to the general public by using advanced technology and by soliciting donations to subsidize its general publishing costs.

Your generosity can help Sophia Institute Press® to provide the public with editions of works containing the enduring wisdom of the ages. Please send your tax-deductible contribution to the address below.

The members of the Editorial Board of Sophia Institute Press® welcome questions, comments, and suggestions from all our readers.

For your free catalog, call:
Toll-free: 1-800-888-9344

or write:
Sophia Institute Press®
Box 5284
Manchester, NH 03108

Internet users may visit our website at
http://www.sophiainstitute.com